Jade Christine Angelica, MDiv

We Are Not Alone
A Teenage Girl's Personal Account of Incest from Disclosure Through Prosecution and Treatment

*Pre-publication
REVIEWS,
COMMENTARIES,
EVALUATIONS . . .*

"**W**e Are Not Alone is a must read for all who work or live with kids who have been ˈ ˈt explores abuse thr˷   ˎ victims,
ˈˈ   wishes.
                                 ˈo meet
                                 ˈstions,
                                 ˈ from
                                 is of-
                                 ˌo them
                                 ˌˌˈerstand.
            ˌˌɩ Alone highlights the fact
 ˌˌ ɩo those of us who work with abused kids, it is our job; but to the kids, it is their life. We must never forget that. *We Are Not Alone* helps us realize that we are also not alone, and that is a great thing. We must all work together to end abuse, and this wonderful book offers tremendous insights into kids and how best to achieve that goal."

"**I**n *We Are Not Alone*, Jade Chri. Angelica provides a valuable source to teens who have been sexuˌ abused and their parents. With compˌ sion and eloquent prose, she walks people through the criminal justice system—from disclosure to final outcome. I believe that her book will be a lifeline to families of teens who have disclosed sexual abuse."

Kathleen Kendall-Tackett, PhD
*Research Associate,
Family Research Laboratory,
University of New Hampshire,
Durham*

Kevin L. Ryle, JD
*Assistant District Attorney,
Middlesex, Massachusetts*

More pre-publication
REVIEWS, COMMENTARIES, EVALUATIONS . . .

"I have the utmost gratitude and praise for Jade Christine Angelica's *We Are Not Alone* guidebook and companion workbooks. They are long-awaited comprehensive and compelling resources for victims and families involved in the child protection and criminal justice systems and the many professionals who work to assist and support them. As a professional working in victim services for almost twenty years, I know how complex and intimidating the system is for victims of all ages and their families. It is particularly daunting for children and adolescents, since the criminal justice system was not designed to meet their unique physical, emotional, and developmental needs. The guidebook points out the harsh realities of the system, but also clearly and sensitively highlights the strides that the child protection and criminal justice systems have made over the past two decades and the efforts to prevent those systems from re-victimizing those they seek to protect. True, the systems are complicated to navigate, but the author is extremely successful in demystifying the system and informing the reader of the positive ways in which the system can and does respond. She strongly encourages victims and their families to participate in the system in an effort to heal from their victimization, seek justice, and hold offenders accountable for their heinous and harmful crimes.

The guidebook is useful not only for victims and their families, but also for professionals working with teen victims and participating as members of multidisciplinary teams. With high staff turnover in many of the agencies involved, this is an exceedingly vital training tool as well. And, of course, the workbooks provide the means by which to engage adolescents in their own care—supporting them in the aftermath of their victimization, helping them engage in quiet introspection, guiding their interactions and conversations with helping professionals and family members, and assisting them to gain the courage necessary to participate in the criminal justice system. Ultimately, these publications will enable them to achieve the goals of vindication, justice, and healing."

Janet E. Fine, MS
Director,
Victim Witness Assistance Program
and Children's Advocacy Center,
Suffolk County District Attorney's Office,
Boston

HMTP

The Haworth Maltreatment and Trauma Press®
An Imprint of The Haworth Press, Inc.
New York • London • Oxford

We Are Not Alone
A Teenage Girl's Personal Account of Incest from Disclosure Through Prosecution and Treatment

We Are Not Alone
A Teenage Girl's Personal Account of Incest from Disclosure Through Prosecution and Treatment

Jade Christine Angelica, MDiv

HMTP

The Haworth Maltreatment and Trauma Press®
An Imprint of The Haworth Press, Inc.
New York • London • Oxford

Published by

The Haworth Maltreatment and Trauma Press®, an imprint of The Haworth Press, Inc., 10 Alice Street, Binghamton, NY 13904-1580

PUBLISHER'S NOTE
All of the characters in the *We Are Not Alone* workbooks are fictitious. Any resemblance to actual persons, living or dead, or events in their lives, is entirely coincidental.

Cover design by Jennifer M. Gaska.

Library of Congress Cataloging-in-Publication Data

Angelica, Jade C. (Jade Christine), 1952-
    We are not alone: a teenage girl's personal account of incest from disclosure through prosecution and treatment / Jade Christine Angelica.
        p. cm.
    ISBN 0-7890-0926-9 (soft : alk paper)
    1. Incest victims—Massachusetts. 2. Sexually abused teenagers—Massachusetts. 3. Trials (Incest)—Massachusetts. 4. Incest victims—Massachusetts. 4. Rehabilitation. I. Title.

HV6570.8.M4 A54 2001
364.15'36—dc21
[B]
                                                                    2001016806

For Chrissie,

With compassion for your suffering
and reverence for your vulnerability.

I am humbled by your resilience
and awed by your commitment to healing.

ABOUT THE AUTHOR

Jade Christine Angelica, MDiv, Director of The Child Abuse Ministry, has been working on behalf of victims of child sexual abuse since 1987. A graduate of Harvard Divinity School, Ms. Angelica leads workshops and training sessions for religious leaders and communities, develops programs and conferences, preaches, lectures, and writes on the topic of child sexual abuse. From 1989 to 1993, Ms. Angelica researched and developed special projects for the Child Abuse Unit of the Middlesex County District Attorney's Office in Cambridge, Massachusetts. In order to provide a sorely needed court-oriented resource for adolescent victims of child sexual abuse, Ms. Angelica wrote the first edition of *We Are Not Alone: A Teenage Girl's Personal Account of Incest Through Prosecution and Treatment,* which was printed in 1992 with a grant from the Massachusetts Bar Association.

Also during her time at the Child Abuse Unit, Ms. Angelica realized the importance of involving faith communities and religious leaders in the multidisciplinary efforts of prevention and healing of child sexual abuse. She is also the author of *A Moral Emergency: Breaking the Cycle of Child Sexual Abuse,* a handbook for religious leaders.

CONTENTS

Introduction

Renee Brant

I am honored to introduce you to *We Are Not Alone,* a sensitive rendering of a teenage girl's experience in the criminal justice system. You will soon meet Jane, a sixteen-year-old girl who was sexually abused by her father. In the wake of her disclosure she meets many professionals. Each has a role to play in the complicated drama that unfolds as Jane tells school administrators and protective service personnel what happened, begins therapy, and winds her way through the criminal justice process.

The author, Jade Angelica, based Jane's saga on the accounts of many teenagers who generously shared their experiences with her. A "child-friendly" and healing spirit permeates *We Are Not Alone,* and I commend Ms. Angelica for her remarkable capacity to empathize with and learn from the teenagers she interviewed. She translated their experiences into a most readable narrative. In addition, *We Are Not Alone* provides examples from actual encounters with dedicated professionals who labor daily on the "front lines" offering protection, comfort, therapy, support, and legal representation to victimized children and their families.

Contact between children and teenagers and the criminal justice system increased significantly in Massachusetts in 1983 following the passage of the new Child Abuse Reporting Law. This law required the Department of Social Services to report certain cases of severe child abuse and child sexual assault to the district attorney's office. As a result, a tremendous influx of cases involving child and teenage victims poured into the criminal justice system. The unique

---

Renee Brant, MD, is the founder of the Sexual Abuse Treatment Team, Children's Hospital, Boston, and is in private practice in child and adolescent psychiatry in Newton, Massachusetts.

1

needs of young victims challenged professionals working within the system. These professionals rose to this challenge by developing specialized, interdisciplinary child abuse protection teams and units such as the Middlesex County Child Abuse Division within the Family Protection Unit of the District Attorney's Office.

The people and systems interacting with sexually abused children have a significant impact on these young victims. Those professionals involved in child abuse investigation, protection, and prosecution can become a part of the problem if they are insensitive to the needs of child and teen victims and their families. In Jane's case, however, the child-friendly and knowledgeable helping professionals she met played a significant role in her healing and recovery. Nothing can undo the trauma of child sexual abuse. However, victimized children and adolescents can have a contrasting and profoundly healing experience in relationships with adults when the adults are attentive to the victims' needs, protective of their vulnerabilities, empathetic to their feelings, and validating of their experiences. Thus, in the best of circumstances, professionals can offer child and adolescent victims a trustworthy, respectful relationship which can help them overcome the isolation, shame, and stigma of sexual abuse.

We Are Not Alone serves multiple purposes. It is a resource for teenagers who are facing the unknowns of the criminal justice system. It provides a guide that introduces teenagers to the key players and procedures of the legal process, and a map for them to follow as they travel through the justice system. It also offers teenagers a peer, Jane, with whose thoughts, feelings, and reactions they can identify.

The central message of *We Are Not Alone* is its title. Teenagers reading this book will hopefully experience connections on various levels. They will learn about the network of professionals who are available to help and support them, and they will have a means of identifying with other teenagers who have traveled this difficult road. Through Jane's experiences, teenagers who have been sexually abused will find a path to realizing and understanding their own feelings and perceptions. They will find a comfort in knowing that "we are not alone."

Welcome to the Teen Reader

Dear Reader,

We Are Not Alone was written specifically for teenagers who have been sexually abused and are involved in the prosecution process. However, adults—including parents, relatives, therapists and social workers, doctors, lawyers, judges and other legal professionals, ministers, priests and rabbis, teachers and school administrators—will also find this resource book informative and helpful in their efforts to support and guide teenage victims of child sexual abuse. If you would like supportive adults in your life to have more information about what you are experiencing in the court system, please ask them to read this book.

We Are Not Alone describes the step-by-step process that Jane, a teenager who was sexually abused by her father for almost ten years, experienced in the Massachusetts superior court system. On page 84, "How It Happened for Me: A Diagram," illustrates a "typical" superior court process. This diagram should be used only as a guideline, because the actual court process will vary from case to case. The legal process and the support systems will also vary from place to place. Each state and county develops and implements its procedures based on particular needs and available resources. Therefore, try to use *We Are Not Alone* as a springboard for helping you understand how systems operate in your county or state.

Some of the words and phrases used in the legal system may be unfamiliar to you. Therefore, a **glossary,** which begins on page 85, has been included. Definitions of the words and phrases found in **bold type** within the text are listed alphabetically in the glossary.

As well as describing the legal process, *We Are Not Alone* highlights some of the feelings and reactions experienced by teenagers who are involved in legal proceedings. Not all teenagers will experience things in the exact way Jane does. Again, her feelings and reactions represent the "typical." Actual feelings and reactions will vary according to each individual. At the end of the book is a section of **guiding questions.** This section is divided by chapter. Thinking about and answering these questions may help you identify and better understand your own feelings and reactions.

Jane's personal account of incest, from disclosure through prosecution, can be read like a novel, from beginning to end. Or, you may prefer to read only the parts that are of particular interest to you. Each section title describes the information covered in that section so you can easily locate topics of specific interest.

Jane expresses some intense emotions. Therefore, the account of her experience may be difficult and upsetting to read at times. If it becomes too distressing, put the book down for awhile. You can always come back to it later. But even if it is hard, do try to keep reading at your own pace. Having detailed information about the legal system will make the difficult process seem less overwhelming and less frightening.

In many ways, Jane's account presents an idealistic scenario of what happens after a child or a teenager discloses details of sexual abuse. Some child and teen victims who have been sexually abused do receive support from their families just as Jane receives from her mom. However, not all victims are so fortunate. The legal system is designed to provide some support—so young victims don't feel all alone—but it is important for victims to also seek the additional support of relatives, friends, other caring adults, and a qualified therapist.

We Are Not Alone is the result of observations of and interviews with professionals in the legal, victim witness, and mental health fields, as well as conversations with and observations of teen victims of sexual abuse and their families. Although Jane's account is fictitious, the spirit of the actual victims and the helping professionals I met is alive in this narrative.

My goal in researching and writing *We Are Not Alone* was to help people learn about child sexual abuse and the legal system. I had no idea that being in the presence of children and teenagers who had been sexually abused and their families would teach me invaluable and life-changing lessons. It has been an honor for me to be with you all.

Identification of Characters

Mr. Burger: The district attorney on *Perry Mason,* the television show.

Dr. Catherine Clayton (Cathy): Jane's therapist.

Dan: Jane's high school friend.

Ms. Feldman: Jane's high school guidance counselor.

Joy: Jane's high school friend.

Andrea Kane: The victim witness advocate from the district attorney's office who worked with Jane and her family throughout the prosecution process.

Lisa Lance-White: The child interview specialist from the district attorney's office who met with Jane and conducted the investigative interviews.

Mr. McCarthy: The defense attorney for Jane's father.

Patricia O'Neill (Patty): The DSS (Department of Social Services) social worker who investigated Jane's disclosure of sexual abuse.

Detective Anthony Rapucci: The local police officer who was part of the team that investigated the allegations against Jane's father.

Nina Santiago: The assistant district attorney who was in charge of prosecuting the case against Jane's father.

Tree-Girl: Jane's cat, who likes to climb trees!

Mrs. Winston: The school nurse at Jane's high school. The first person Jane told about the sexual abuse.

Section 1

I'm Jane

My name is Jane. I'm sixteen years old and a junior in high school. From the time I was a little girl, about five years old, I guess, my father was sexually abusing me. And until I saw a video at school in ninth grade, I didn't even know it was "abuse." I always felt pretty weird about it, you know, scared, ashamed, and sick to my stomach a lot, but Dad told me it was OK. It was "good," he said, because I was "special," and he loved me "so much." Even though it hurt me sometimes, I thought he was loving me, not abusing me.

And then I saw this video about sexual abuse in my health science class at school. I knew for sure, right then, that what my dad was doing was wrong. I felt really confused, dirty, and scared. Oh, I felt stupid, too. Stupid and mad at myself because I didn't know what was happening.

I didn't know what to do, but I just kept getting more and more upset inside. I was nervous all the time. I cried a lot and had headaches every single day. I was really tired because I was so nervous I couldn't sleep at night. I didn't want to talk to any of my friends or go to school anymore. But I did. I did everything as usual. I kept pretending, like always, that everything in my life was just fine. It was the worst feeling.

I was truly confused. I didn't want to tell Dad to stop because I didn't want to hurt his feelings, and I didn't know if he would stop anyway. I didn't want to tell him that I knew he was abusing me, and I especially didn't want him to think that I didn't love him anymore. Besides, what we did felt really good sometimes. I liked getting the attention from my dad. I was afraid to tell Mom because I didn't think she'd believe me, or if she did, I was afraid she would blame me. I was afraid that nobody would believe me, and everyone would blame me. I was so scared all the time, that finally I prayed to God to help me, just because I didn't know who else to ask.

Section 2

The First Time I Told

One day at school, about three weeks after I first saw the video, I was really tired and feeling very sick. So after lunch period, I went to the school nurse's office and asked Mrs. Winston, the nurse, if I could rest for awhile. I guess I looked pretty bad, because she wanted to send me home. Since my mom works downtown and didn't have the car, Mrs. Winston asked me for my dad's telephone number at work so he could come and pick me up.

I don't know what happened to me, but I couldn't move, and I couldn't talk either. I sat like I was frozen, just staring at the floor. And I remember hot, stinging tears. They started pouring out of my eyes, but I still didn't make a sound. I covered my face with my hands, and cried for what seemed like forever.

Mrs. Winston sat next to me, patiently handing me tissue after tissue. When I finally started to stop crying, Mrs. Winston quietly asked, "Jane, can you tell me what's wrong?"

And I just said it. In between quivering sobs and hiccups, I whispered, "Mrs. Winston, my dad has sex with me . . . like in the video we saw." For a very long minute after I said it, the whole room was so quiet and still, I thought for sure the world had ended. But it didn't. I was still there. Mrs. Winston was still there.

Mrs. Winston got me a glass of water. As I sipped it, she told me that she believed me and wanted to help me. She told me what happened with my dad wasn't my fault, and that I was a really "brave young woman" for telling her.

I don't know if I can describe how I felt then, because I felt all mixed up for sure, but I'll try. I felt relief because I didn't have to carry the heavy burden of the "special secret" all alone anymore. I felt grateful to Mrs. Winston for believing me, and for being so nice to me. I felt guilty because I didn't want my dad to get in trouble or my mom to be upset. I felt so very scared that my dad and mom would be really mad at me for making trouble for them, and that they wouldn't want to be my parents anymore. And I felt so ashamed. I felt dirty and used, and I wanted to hide so no one would see me, so no one would know.

I was surprised to learn that my high school had standard procedures for handling the **disclosure** of sexual abuse. Mrs. Winston said it was her responsibility to call **DSS** (The Department of Social Services), to report what I had told her. She said she would also like to have my guidance counselor, Ms. Feldman, come to be with me.

Ms. Feldman came right away, but I couldn't talk to her. I couldn't even look at her. I stared at the floor wishing I could disappear, wishing I was at home watching TV and eating cookies. It was too hard, too horrible, too embarrassing to talk about.

Then Mrs. Winston called DSS to file an official report because of the **mandated reporting law.** As the school nurse, Mrs. Winston is considered a **mandated reporter.** That means she has a legal responsibility to report incidents or disclosures or suspicions of abuse of children to DSS. So when you tell someone who is a mandated reporter, like a teacher, or a doctor, or a counselor, they will help you. That's the law.

Section 3

Making a Report

While Mrs. Winston was filing the report with a **social worker** over the telephone, my guidance counselor explained some things to me about what would happen next. Even though I could not look at her, and could not really even listen to her, she explained anyway. Ms. Feldman told me that she wanted me to have all the information. She said, "Once the report is received and evaluated, a social worker will be assigned to your case. Then DSS will have ten days to investigate." Although they legally had ten days to investigate, Ms. Feldman said that a social worker might be in touch with me sooner.

"These next several days might be particularly stressful for you, Jane," Ms. Feldman said, "and you may have a hard time being at home." Then she gave me this telephone number for a twenty-four-hour **crisis line,** "just in case" I needed to talk to someone. Ms. Feldman said she was trying to prepare me for what was going to happen and how I might feel about it.

She was so encouraging and so nice, and I appreciated her efforts even though I couldn't tell her so at the time. But unfortunately, nothing could have helped me feel better on that day. I was too upset and too confused to be consoled. I needed to think.

Because of my particular circumstances, Mrs. Winston and Ms. Feldman thought it would be best if my parents didn't know about my disclosure until my social worker was involved. So I stayed in the nurse's office for the rest of the day, feeling numb and very stupid, and then I went home.

I went right to my room and turned on the radio—loud! I was so confused and frightened that I just sat and stared out the window through the trees, into the sky. I felt as nervous as Tree-Girl, our cat, who was keeping me company by pacing around my room. I actually jumped out of my chair when I heard the front door close, and Mom yelled, "I'm home." While Mom made dinner, I paced with Tree-Girl, twisting my fingers until they were purple and numb beyond hurting. I didn't know what to do. I felt like I was being torn in two. Part of me felt so relieved that I had told, and part of me wished I had never said a word.

Dad came home, and we all ate dinner. I didn't say much. Everything seemed just the same as usual, except inside me. I was different inside. I knew inside that it was over, and I was so thankful. But I was really, really scared about what would happen next. And I was sad. I looked at Dad across the table, and realized how much I loved him, and how much he loved me. My dad had such a way of making me feel special.

After dinner I watched TV because it was the only thing that I could do.

Section 4

The Investigation Begins

The hardest part of the whole **investigation** and **prosecution** process was having to wait and at the same time not knowing what was going to happen to me, to Dad, and to our family. I cried every time I thought that Dad might not be sitting at the dinner table with us anymore. But I didn't even want to think about that.

Fortunately, at the beginning, I didn't have to wait for very long before things began to happen. It was only three days later, although it seemed like an eternity, when Ms. Feldman called me into the Guidance Office. She told me my DSS social worker, Patricia O'Neill, would like to meet with me the next day at school. Ms. Feldman said it would be best if my mom could be here, too. So she called Mom at work and asked her to come to my school for an important meeting.

At 9:00 a.m. the next morning, I met Patricia O'Neill in the counseling center at school. I was totally nervous from not knowing what to expect. Ms. O'Neill was very nice, and she tried to calm me down. She said I could call her "Patty."

Patty began our meeting by asking me if I knew why she was there to see me. I knew all right, but it was hard to answer her. She repeated the question, "Jane, do you know why I'm here this morning?"

"Because of my dad," I whispered. "Because I told Mrs. Winston that my dad has sex with me."

"Yes, Jane. That is why I'm here."

And then Patty explained her role as my DSS social worker and the procedures that would happen next. When she finished talking it was almost 10:00. She said she was going to meet with my mom, and invited me to be in the room if I wanted. I decided to wait in Ms. Feldman's office until after they told Mom.

Patty told me I was very brave, which took me completely by surprise because I felt so scared. But I guess in order to be brave, you have to be scared first.

As Patty got up to leave the room, I looked at her, and I said, "I need to ask you a very important question."

She sat right back down, looked at me, and said, "OK, shoot."

I looked right into her eyes when I asked, "Why did my dad do this to me?"

Patty was real quiet for a minute, and then she said, "I know this isn't a very good answer, Jane, but it's the only true answer I know right now." She took a very deep breath, kind of like a sigh, and continued, "The truth is, I do not know why your father did this. But I do know you did the right thing by telling us. So now we can protect you, and help your mom and your dad. Your dad really needs help so he doesn't hurt you or any other kids ever again."

I just nodded in response.

Then Patty shook my hand. That made me feel very grown-up and important. She gave me her business card with her office telephone number and address. She said that I could call her anytime if I had questions, or if I wanted to talk to her. Then Patty went to meet with my mom.

I looked at her card for a long time, just thinking about things, I guess. Finally, I put the card in my backpack, and nervously waited for Ms. Feldman to come for me.

Section 5

I'm Sorry, Mom

About twenty minutes later, the longest twenty minutes of my life, I think, Ms. Feldman came to get me so I could talk to Patty and Mom. I went into the room, and I could see right away that Mom had been crying. I sat down next to her, and she took my hand. I said, "I'm really sorry, Mom."

She hugged me and said, "Oh no, Janie, I'm sorry." She started to cry again.

I guess Mom was pretty shocked and upset because she didn't say much else. It was a good thing that Patty and Ms. Feldman were calm and knew what to do.

Patty said something had to be done to keep me safe from my father. She told Mom that either I had to stay with someone else—she suggested a foster family—or Dad had to leave our house. Mom asked Patty what would be best for me. Patty said it would be best if Dad left so I could stay in my own home with my mom. I was happy to hear that because I didn't want to be alone or with strangers. I was too upset to adjust to that. Mom said that Dad could stay with his brother, my Uncle John. Everyone agreed that would be best. I was so relieved. But sad, too. Like I worried before, I wouldn't see Dad at dinner anymore, and he wouldn't be there to make me feel special. Then I started to cry.

Mom agreed to call Dad at work before she left my school. She asked for Ms. Feldman or Patty to stay with her while she made the call.

Then Patty told us that it might be helpful for me to talk with a **counselor** who works with kids my age. She said, "It's a good idea for kids who have been sexually abused to be able to talk with someone about what happened. And, Jane, you also might need to talk with someone about what's happening now and how you feel about it all."

Patty suggested that Mom might be interested in going with me to the counselor for awhile. Mom took the paper with the referral on it and quietly said, "Thank you." I wondered what would become of that name and telephone number. Mom didn't really believe too much in counselors.

Then Patty started to talk about a meeting she wanted to have, which she called a **team interview.** She wanted Mom's permission to schedule it as soon as possible, which to Patty meant within the next day or two. She explained, "This interview is part of the DSS investigation, and it's done in the team format so Jane won't have to be interviewed too many times by too many different people. Not all places use a team interview because they think other ways are better, but we always use the team interview here because we think it is easier on the kids to only have to say what happened one time during this part of the investigation."

I remember just staring at Patty when she said "easier." Like anything could make this easier.

Patty continued, "For the team interview, we gather all the people who need to know what happened. That's me as the investigative social worker for DSS, the **assistant district attorney,** the **victim witness advocate,** the **child interview specialist,** a police officer, and a **therapist** from a local mental health clinic."

I almost had a heart attack when I realized I would have to say what my dad did in front of all those people, but Patty calmed me down right away.

She said, "You actually only have to tell one person at the **interview,** and that will be the child interview specialist. The others will observe the interview from behind a two-way mirror. They will be able to see and hear you, Jane, but you won't be able to see or hear them."

Well, that sounded a bit better, but I didn't like the idea of telling anyone else. I didn't want more people to know. It was embarrassing enough already, and the more people who knew, the more embarrassed I felt. I mean, really. What was going to happen if the kids at school found out? They would think I was easy, and some slut, you know. I was afraid none of the guys would ever ask me out. Oh, this was so terrible. I felt so dirty. I wanted to disappear.

But Patty said if we were going to stop this abuse from happening to me, we needed to do the team interview. It was nice that she said "WE." I didn't feel so alone.

I was nervous and upset about this, of course, but Mom said, "Yes" right away. She said, "Yes, we need to protect Jane. Please schedule the interview as soon as possible. Jane and I will be there."

Believe it or not, I wanted to go to my classes that day. I needed a distraction. I wanted to feel "regular" for a few hours, or even for a few minutes. Even if I was just pretending again, that was OK.

Mom said it was fine for me to go to class. She said she would call Dad and ask him to pick up his things before I got home from school.

I say felt "nervous," but that's only because I don't know of a word that describes how completely upset I was. I don't know what Mom said to Dad, but when I got home he wasn't there. Mom told me that Dad said I had misunderstood his gestures, that he was merely being really affectionate. Dad wondered where I got such a "silly notion" that he was abusing me. I got that numb feeling again and stared at the floor. I didn't feel, think, or say anything. I just knew I needed my mom to believe me.

Section 6

The Interview

About 5:30 p.m. that same afternoon, Patty O'Neill called from DSS to let us know about the team interview. It was scheduled for 3:00 p.m. the next day at the district attorney's office. They have a special Child Unit set up there to handle all the child abuse cases in the county.

Mom and I arrived at the office at about five minutes past 3:00. We were late because I kept changing my clothes. I knew it didn't make much sense to care about what I was wearing, but I was just so nervous. Patty met us at the door, and tried to make us feel comfortable. Seeing her familiar face made me feel safe somehow.

The team was already meeting in a big conference room which had a very long table and lots of chairs. Then this woman, Lisa, came out into the reception area where Mom and I were waiting. Lisa was my interviewer. When she shook my hand I did manage to look at her face. I was surprised to see that she looked very friendly. She said, "Hi, Jane." And she smiled at me.

I said, "Hello," and looked quickly down at the floor.

After a few minutes, Lisa and I went into a small very neat room. In the room were two chairs, a small table, sort of like a coffee table, this huge mirror that covered one whole wall, and a box of tissues. It was weird. You know, sort of uncomfortable to see myself in the mirror. I felt a little self-conscious. Lisa explained that the people from the team were on the other side of the mirror, and they could see and hear us. She said she thought it might be easier for me to talk with only her in the room.

Before the interview started, Lisa explained why certain people needed to observe. She said, "Patty O'Neill will be observing as a part of her investigation for DSS. In her report, Patty needs to indicate whether or not she **supports the allegations** of the sexual abuse.

Nina Santiago, the assistant district attorney assigned to your case, will be making **prosecution** decisions, and the victim witness advocate, Andrea Kane, will be making assessments about your emotional readiness to be a witness in court."

I wasn't sure what all of that meant, but I was sure this interview was very important. As hard as it was for me to talk about the sexual abuse, I knew I had to tell the truth. I didn't want Dad to hurt me anymore.

Then Lisa started asking questions. It helped me sometimes to close my eyes as I answered.

"Can you talk a little louder, Jane? You're whispering."

"Yes," I replied, opening my eyes. "I can talk louder."

I sat up straighter in my chair and opened my eyes. I needed to focus in order to do this.

Then Lisa asked me to tell exactly what Dad did. I didn't say it all, I could never say it all. But I made myself say some of it. Saying the words, "penis" and "vagina," talking about my dad and me, made me feel so ashamed and guilty. I'm quite sure I mumbled a lot. I'm very sure I stared at the floor a lot. I noticed some scratches on my shoes and a piece of navy blue thread on the floor. Lisa's shoes were black suede. And then I started to cry. I covered my eyes with my hands, and Lisa handed me the box of tissues. She told me it was definitely OK to cry, and so I did.

Lisa was very understanding about me being so upset. Like Patty and Mrs. Winston did, Lisa told me I was very brave. I looked at her, I remember, feeling confused, because I didn't feel especially brave at that moment. But buried somewhere beneath the confusion and the upset, I did feel proud of myself for being strong enough to do something that was so scary.

After the interview and after the tears, Lisa explained what would happen next. She said that if Mom and I wanted to talk with my team today, we could wait in the reception area while the team reviewed my interview. We could meet with them today or later, separately or together. There was "no pressure," she said. It was totally my choice. Mom and I talked it over, and we decided to stay and meet my team.

Section 7

After the Interview

I wandered around the reception area for about twenty minutes while Mom tried to be calm and read a magazine. I felt best about meeting the team with Mom in the room, so when Lisa came to get me, Mom and I went into the big conference room together. It was hard to be with all these people because I felt ashamed that they knew such private things about me. It was a struggle for me to even look at them.

All the people on the team explained their job responsibilities to me, and what would happen next. It was hard for me to understand everything they said. Mostly, it was hard for me to even listen because I was so distracted by my own upset and embarrassment. But everyone was nice to me, and it was clear they were used to working with kids and knew what they were doing. I really got the feeling that they were all on my side.

Patty spoke first. "Based on your interview, Jane, there is enough evidence to support the allegations of child sexual abuse in my report for DSS." Then the Assistant District Attorney, Nina Santiago, talked about the prosecution process. She explained, "With your testimony, Jane, there appears to be enough evidence to proceed with the criminal prosecution of your father. The Commonwealth of Massachusetts will file the charges against him in **superior court.** You will not actually be responsible for taking your dad to court. But in order for the case to go forward, you need to be willing to be a **witness.** Your initial testimony will be videotaped so you won't have to testify live, in person, in front of all the people of the **grand jury.**"

"What's a grand jury?" I asked.

Nina replied, "It's a jury of citizens who consider evidence brought before the superior court and decide if there is cause to believe a crime has been committed."

I told her that I had never heard of a "grand jury."

And so, Nina explained more about it. She said that not all states have grand juries, and in those states, the **probable cause hearing** takes place before a judge. She also said that sometimes the states that do have grand juries don't use them for child abuse cases. "It is one of those legal procedures which really varies from state to state, " she said. "And since we do have the grand jury here, we have to present the evidence for your case to them. The videotaping of your **testimony** will hopefully make that part of the process easier for you, Jane. But if the case goes to trial, you need to be able and willing to **testify** in court."

This information and my emotions were somewhat overwhelming. Although my team was very nice, they were also very serious about wanting my dad to take responsibility for what he did. I asked what would happen to Dad if the case went forward.

My victim witness advocate, Andrea Kane, replied. She said, "There are a variety of possible **dispositions** of a criminal case, Jane, and if your dad is found **guilty,** Nina and I will talk with you and your mom about what you want to happen before we make a recommendation to the court."

While Andrea was talking, I couldn't keep my eyes off the police officer, Detective Rapucci. I wasn't planning to say anything to him but I just blurted out the question, "Are you going to arrest my father?" I was very upset about the possibility of Dad being in jail! I don't know if I felt ashamed, sad, scared, or guilty about that possibility, but I knew I WAS UPSET!

Detective Rapucci assured me he would not be arresting my dad at this time. He said, "I might ask your dad some questions, but I will discuss every detail of the investigation with the assistant district attorney to decide whether an arrest should be made."

Andrea continued the conversation. "There will be lots of time to talk about what might happen to your dad, and your feelings about what could happen will certainly be considered."

The next person to speak was the therapist from the mental health clinic. She said, "It's clear that this experience is upsetting for Jane, and under these circumstances, upset is a perfectly normal reaction."

I was relieved to be considered "normal." But then I started to cry because she went on to say that it might be helpful for me to talk with a counselor. Everybody, including my mom, nodded.

I was confused. And angry. A second ago I was "normal," and now I felt like there was something really wrong with me because they wanted me to go to a counselor. I wondered if maybe these people thought I was crazy. I asked, angry about it, and they all said they didn't think I was crazy. Patty reminded me how important it would be for me to talk about my feelings and fears with someone I trusted.

Mom mentioned that we had an appointment in a few days with the therapist Patty O'Neill had recommended. That surprised me. Mom said that she made the appointment the same day Patty gave her the number. Patty said, "It's good to know that there will be an additional support person in Jane's life during this difficult time."

Mom asked if she and I could have a few minutes alone together to talk things over, so everyone left the room. Mom said that she knew a public trial would for sure be a hard experience for our family, and especially hard for me. "But," she said, "protecting you is my primary concern, Janie. And, it's important to keep your father away from other kids." She also said, "We need to make sure your dad gets help."

I just nodded.

When the team returned, Mom told them that we would cooperate with the district attorney's office in preparing the case against Dad for trial. They were all very businesslike as, one by one, they thanked us.

Before we left the office, Andrea scheduled an appointment for me to come back in a few weeks to videotape the interview of my testimony for the grand jury. Then she gave me her business card, and told me I could call her if I had any questions about the legal process, or didn't understand something that happened, or even if I just wanted to talk to somebody. I put her card in my backpack along with Patty's. Having their telephone numbers with me all the time helped me to feel protected.

Then, as we were leaving the office, Andrea said, "I'll be in touch with you very soon, Jane. Just remember, it's my job to answer any and all of your questions, explain the court process, provide support to you and your mom, and to keep you notified of the case status. I had hoped to explain the court process to you this afternoon, but that seems like it might be too much for one day. So, we'll do that another time, OK?"

That was fine with me. My mind was spinning.

Then Andrea reassured me that she would be there for me. And I believed her.

Section 8

Counseling

I went to school the next couple days, and being there was a relief. I wanted to forget about Dad and what was happening to me and my family. Pretending everything was OK had become a way of life for me, and although pretending was harder now, I was still pretty good at it.

I had not told any of my friends or teachers or anyone what was going on, and that was becoming a problem for me. Not telling was making me feel isolated and alone. I wanted some of my friends to know because I really wanted people to understand me. You know, I wanted them to feel sad with me, and I wanted them to feel angry with me, too. Really, I just didn't want to feel alone with all of this.

But I didn't know who to tell. I didn't know who to trust because sometimes kids can be so mean to each other, even kids who you think are your friends. Last year this one girl had an abortion and some other girls left signs on her locker and in the girl's room calling her a baby killer. That was so mean. I'm sure she did what she thought was the best thing for her to do. But when I imagined what they might say about me, I actually thought I would throw up. Oh, and thinking that the boys would find out. Oh no! I couldn't even think about that! I felt so ashamed.

Mom and I went together to see the counselor Patty O'Neill recommended. Her name was Dr. Catherine Clayton, but she said I could call her "Cathy." I liked that. During our first session, I couldn't talk much about anything. I cried a lot, but that seemed OK with Mom and Cathy. We all decided I could come by myself to the next session which we scheduled for two days later.

When Mom and I were leaving, Cathy gave me her business card with her telephone number on it. She told me I could call her any time, day or night, if I wanted to talk to her . . . or if I wanted her to talk to me. I kind of smiled as I put her card into my backpack along with Patty's and Andrea's. I felt like I had a whole team of people in there helping me to get through this.

During my next appointment with Cathy I was calmer, for some unknown reason, and I felt more prepared. I had a list of things I wanted to talk about. I had my questions written on a piece of paper that was folded about thirty times and stuffed into the inside pocket of my jacket.

First on my list was what to do about feeling so isolated. I still had not told anyone. Although I didn't want to feel so alone, I also didn't want anyone else to know.

Second on the list was the feeling of being ruined for life, worrying that no boys would ever go out with me because they would think I was dirty and all used up already. I felt like maybe I was bad in some way because a lot of time the sex and the physical closeness felt good to me.

I was really afraid about what the sexual abuse had done to my body. I wondered if I wouldn't be able to have children, or if maybe I had AIDS or some other disease. I was so sure people could tell I'd been having sex just by looking at me. I wanted to hide, or be invisible, maybe.

I also wanted to talk about my dad, my mom, and my family. When I got to that number on my list of questions, tears started to seep out of my eyes. I tried to blink them back inside me, but I couldn't. I missed my dad. And I was very confused because Dad kept calling me to tell me how much he loved me. I asked Cathy, "Does he really love me? Why did he do this? Why did he ruin our family? Why did he hurt me? And Mom? He hurt Mom, too. And why did he lie and say I misunderstood?" This was just too hard. I kept wishing it had never happened.

Then I managed to tell Cathy that I had been feeling so terrible when I was alone at night that I actually thought I might rather be dead than to feel this way. I was having horrible nightmares.

I also wasn't sure if I did the right thing by telling, or if I was doing the right thing by planning to testify. I felt guilty and confused. My dad might go to jail, and maybe it was really my fault like he said. Maybe I did want him to do it. I felt like screaming! Cathy said it was fine to go ahead and scream, but I was too embarrassed.

Cathy listened while I went down my list of questions and concerns, which I read pretty fast, stumbling over my words sometimes. When I finished, I looked up at her and she smiled at me. Then she leaned forward a little bit, closer to me but not too close. She said, "Jane, I can see that you may be feeling really scared and nervous and sad and confused about all of this. And before I say anything else, I want to tell you that it is completely normal to be feeling all of those things."

Normal, again. What a relief. I sighed, and relaxed a little.

Cathy continued. "This is a great list, Jane. I can see that you worked hard putting it together, and I know it took a lot of strength to put your thoughts and feelings onto paper and bring them here." Then she said that dealing with sexual abuse issues was tough, and that it was "a real act of courage" for me to tell Mrs. Winston about my dad.

Cathy also said she was glad I trusted her enough to bring my list to her. She said we would talk about whatever I wanted to whenever I wanted to, whether it was on the list or not. "We can talk about the details of the abuse when you feel ready to do that, Jane. But it's also important for us to talk about your reactions to what is happening in your life right now, as well as your feelings about your family, your friends and your school experiences." It felt good not to be pressured to talk about what Dad did to me.

Unfortunately, Cathy didn't think we'd be able to answer all of my questions in that hour on that day. I was disappointed about that because I wanted answers. "But," she said, "you can tell me where you want to begin, and we will begin."

And so we did. It was really hard to talk about my feelings, but I made myself. Somewhere deep down inside, I knew it was important to get my feelings out of me and into the world. Cathy helped me to talk by asking me direct questions, by listening to my answers, and by being really gentle with me. The hour with Cathy was painful, but it passed quickly. We decided I would come to see her on Mondays and Thursdays for the next month. That way, Cathy said, I wouldn't feel so alone.

Since talking about wanting to die rather than deal with all of this wasn't what I chose from my list to talk about that day, Cathy said she wanted to take some extra time before I left to talk about those feelings. She said, "I suggest that you keep the telephone number of the twenty-four-hour crisis line Ms. Feldman gave you handy at all times. And I encourage you to use it, to talk to someone there, especially another teenager, if you want or need to talk with someone about what happened. Everything you say will be kept private."

Cathy then asked me to promise that the next time I felt so bad, I would call her, no matter what time. She encouraged me to put the crisis line telephone number and her telephone number on a piece of paper right next to my bed, so they would be there for me at night when I felt so scared and alone.

Section 9

Prosecution Begins

The next week my victim witness advocate, Andrea Kane, called from the district attorney's office. She said that she wanted to follow up on our meeting and to answer any questions I might have. She also wanted to explain the investigation, interview, and court processes to me.

But before doing any of that, Andrea asked, "How are you feeling, Jane? How is your therapy going?"

I didn't say much.

So then Andrea said, "I understand that this is really hard and painful for you. But remember, the case will only be brought to court if your therapist, your mom, and you think it is advisable for you."

It seemed to me that everyone wanted to make sure I would be OK, and that the court process wouldn't be harmful to me or interfere with my healing process.

Andrea and I confirmed a date for the grand jury interview which involved videotaping my testimony. Then she offered me some options for how to go about discussing some details about the prosecution process. She said, "We can talk on the phone, or meet earlier on the day of the interview, or, you can come into my office for a separate meeting." I decided on the separate meeting, so we scheduled a meeting for the next day after school.

When we got together the next afternoon, Andrea explained that the grand jury consists of a group of citizens who are registered voters in our county. They are called for jury duty for a three-month period, and are assigned to review the evidence for superior court cases. Their job is to hear evidence on serious cases and to determine if the case should go forward into the court system.

Assistant District Attorney Nina Santiago would present the case against my dad to the grand jury, and then they would watch the videotape of my testimony. Dad and his lawyer would not be there. After the presentation of the evidence, the grand jury votes on whether or not they think there is sufficient evidence to prosecute. If they think YES, they issue an **indictment.** If they think, NO, the case is closed.

This sounded like a foreign language to me, and it was all pretty confusing. So confusing actually, that I didn't really know what to ask when Andrea wanted to know if I had any questions.

She went on to explain about the **criminal justice system.** She said, "The criminal justice system is designed to protect the rights of the accused. In this case, that's your dad. He is accused of sexually abusing you." Andrea reminded me of the phrase we learned in junior high civics class, "presumed innocent until proven guilty." She said, "The assistant district attorney must convince a trial **jury,** beyond a **reasonable doubt,** that your dad is guilty of sexually abusing you."

Andrea also said, "The criminal court system is really designed for adults and it is sometimes especially hard for kids. Things can be said, and things can happen that kids don't understand. But I'm always here to help you. Please, just ask me. Anything. Feel free to ask me anything."

Finally I did manage to ask a few questions, just to see if I could make some sense of all that Andrea was saying. Then I realized it would be helpful to write some things down in case I forgot, or so I could think about this and ask more questions later.

Before we ended the conversation, Andrea reminded me again that it was OK for me to call her if I wanted to talk or if I had any questions. I didn't know how to respond to her. I'm not the type to ask a lot of questions, or to call people when I need to talk for fear that I will be bothering them. But it seemed that everyone I met—Patty, Cathy, Andrea—kept inviting me, encouraging me, to call, whenever, and to ask whatever. I began to think that maybe I wouldn't be such a bother after all.

Andrea reminded me again of the grand jury interview scheduled in a few weeks with Lisa. She also reminded me that it would only happen if I felt ready. She assured me I could decide if and when the time was right for the interview. Andrea and Nina, the **ADA,** would be there observing the interview from behind the two-way mirror.

Andrea also said she would call my mom sometime during the next few days to tell her what would happen next and to answer her questions.

"Good-bye, Jane." Andrea said as she walked me to the door of the office. "Take care. And call me. I'm here for you." I felt my eyes swell with tears.

"Good-bye, Andrea. And thanks," I said.

I stood outside the building for a long time, just staring at the puffy, pure white clouds floating through the sky. I felt furious that this was happening to me. Why? Why did I have to deal with this?

Section 10

Pretrial Testimony

Mom and I went together to the district attorney's office on the day of my interview for the grand jury. It had been a hard and painful time for us both. Dad kept calling. He was trying to convince us not to become involved in the legal process. He kept saying how much he loved us, and insisted we could "work things out as a family." But when Dad realized that all the insisting in the world wasn't going to change anything, he tried to convince Mom that the abuse wasn't abuse. And that whatever it was, it was MY fault, not his.

Mom was upset by everything, and she found a therapist to talk to. She was considering a divorce. Dad said that was my fault, too. I wondered if maybe he was right. Cathy told me over and over that the sexual abuse wasn't my fault, and in some ways I could believe that. But I felt that the problems happening in my family were because of me. If only I hadn't told. I was confused but grateful that I had Cathy to help me. She was convinced that I was not to blame for the abuse or for my parents' problems.

Lisa, Andrea, and Nina Santiago were all going to be a part of the interviewing process. Before beginning the taping, they spent some time talking to me, trying to calm me down, I think. Although I felt scared, I also felt like a very important person at a business meeting with other important people. I tried to act especially grown-up, really because I didn't want anyone to know how scared I was.

Andrea asked me how I was feeling.

I said, "Fine."

She asked how my therapy was going and how I liked Cathy.

"Fine. Fine."

Andrea wanted to make sure I would be OK if I gave my testimony that day, and she said that she was happy to hear I would be seeing Cathy later in the afternoon. It was Cathy's idea for me to have an appointment with her after the interview. That way I would feel "supported," she said.

The interview room was the same room I was in before when I talked to Lisa. Everything was just the same, except the navy blue thread had been vacuumed up from the floor. I sat in a chair facing the mirror and the camera hiding behind it. Lisa spoke to the mirror and asked for the camera to be turned on. Andrea and Nina were on the other side of the mirror, so I guess one of them did that.

Lisa spoke to the camera. "Good afternoon. Today is November 16. My name is Lisa Lance-White from the district attorney's office. I'm here today meeting with Jane." Then Lisa spoke to me. "Jane, do you understand that it is important for you to tell the truth when you answer the questions I'm going to ask you today?"

I answered "Yes," but my voice was so soft because there was this huge lump in my throat, that Lisa had to ask me to speak louder. I said it again, "YES."

Then she said, "Do you promise to tell the truth today, Jane?"

I replied, "Yes, I do." I shivered a bit, shut my eyes tight, and took a deep breath. I was really doing this!

Lisa began asking me some simple questions like my full name, my birthday, where I went to school, what grade I was in, my address, and who lives with me. While I was answering those questions, Lisa had to remind me to speak up. I was very nervous, and even laughed a couple times during those first questions. I couldn't believe I laughed, because it definitely wasn't a funny experience, but I was just so nervous. I actually clenched the arms of my chair the whole time, maybe so I wouldn't get up and run away.

And then came the hard questions. Lisa asked, "Jane, did something happen with your father? What happened? When did it begin? How often did it happen? Where did it happen? When did it stop . . . ."

As I answered these questions for Lisa, I remember reaching up to my face, and brushing the tears from my cheeks. My face was so hot. It seemed like I was in the interview room answering these questions forever, and I was really surprised to find out that the whole thing only took about fifteen minutes.

At the end of the interview Lisa thanked me, and she walked with me into the reception area to get my mom. Then we met for a short time in the big conference room. Nina, Andrea, and Lisa said that my testimony was "excellent." But all I cared about, really, was that it was over. I felt so relieved. I just knew I did the right thing.

Andrea said she would call me in a couple of days to discuss the next step. You know what I liked most about Andrea? She always called me when she said she was going to. That made me feel like I could really count on her to be there for me.

When we left the office, Mom took me to McDonald's and bought me a vanilla milk shake. My favorite. Believe me, I really needed that milk shake.

Then I went to see Cathy.

Section 11

Counseling Support

Have I mentioned how tired I was? During those weeks after I first told Mrs. Winston about my dad, I was just so tired all the time. I felt sick a lot, too. And confused. Yes, for sure. I felt tired and sick and confused that afternoon when I went to see Cathy.

You know, I love my dad, and I felt so guilty about what I said about him. And now it was on videotape. A grand jury of the superior court was going to hear what my dad did to me. I was too embarrassed to even think about it. But I was also sad because I didn't really want my dad to get in any trouble. When I saw Cathy I told her I was afraid. I was thinking maybe I shouldn't be involved in this prosecution thing.

Cathy said that she understood my confusion. That afternoon she helped me to understand it, too, and to accept being confused. I just wanted everything in my life to be fine and smooth and simple, and everyone in my family to be happy. I felt like such a troublemaker.

Cathy told me that it was OK to love my dad and to still want him to be responsible for his actions. After all, Dad abused me. "Your father has some problems, Jane, and he needs help," Cathy said. "However," she continued, "what he did to you is a crime. Legally and morally, it is a crime." She explained that the child abuse laws were made to protect me, and that I had a right to be protected. Cathy and everyone at the district attorney's office had a way of making me feel like I was somebody important. Since they believed so strongly that I had "rights," I came to believe it, too.

Patty O'Neill told me, and Lisa told me, and Andrea told me that if testifying felt too hard for me, I could stop the prosecution process at any time. After all, I was the primary witness. Without my cooperation there was really no case. Cathy reminded me again that feeling reluctant about the court process is normal. Then she said, "Know that you do have a choice about testifying, Jane."

I left Cathy's office feeling less tired, but I was definitely lost in thoughts about what she told me. I was "important." I had "rights." I could "choose." I felt better because I felt like I had some control over my life.

Section 12

Waiting

The next few weeks seemed endless because I didn't know what was happening. And mostly it didn't seem that anything was happening. But I guess even though I couldn't see it, the justice system was, in fact, operating.

Some of the time I was kind of in a panic, and I think I called either Andrea or Nina or both of them at least once a day to see how my case was going. I needed to know. Nina was in court a lot, so sometimes she didn't call me back right away and I would panic even more, worrying that she forgot me. But Andrea always called me, and even though she sometimes didn't have much new information, just talking to her helped me to calm down.

Then finally, one day after school, Andrea called. The *Commonwealth vs. My Dad* would be heard by the grand jury the following Tuesday. "And then a couple weeks after that," she said, "we'll know if an indictment will be issued."

I felt a surge of excitement rush through my body, like an electric current up and down my back and legs and arms. But when I hung up the phone I felt stunned. I sat in the living room for a long time waiting for Mom to come home from work. As the sun went down I watched the house get dark and the shadows appear. I never even turned on the lights. Really, I wasn't even sure if I could move. Tree-Girl waited with me. We sat on the couch, watching the shadows. The only sounds I noticed were the ticking of the clock and Tree-Girl's purring. Waiting . . . waiting . . . it seemed like forever.

Section 13

At School

I wanted to go to school—to be distracted mostly—but I also didn't want to go. A few days after the meeting at school with Mom and Patty O'Neill and Ms. Feldman, Mom met with the principal to explain my "situation." The principal then talked with all of my teachers, and without being specific, explained that I was experiencing a family crisis. She told my teachers that I might be late or absent, or sometimes I might have difficulty concentrating, or maybe I would need some extra help with my work or some extra attention. I was embarrassed about this "special" treatment because I didn't want the other kids to notice it and tease me. But down deep, I really appreciated everyone's help and concern. And this truly was a family crisis.

Cathy and Mom helped me decide which of my friends to tell and how to tell them. Cathy also helped to prepare me for their possible reactions. It's hard for some kids to understand about taking your own father to court. I could totally relate, because it was hard for me to understand, too.

Mom helped a lot. She talked to my friends' moms so they could understand what was happening. It felt so weird to me when this secret thing wasn't a secret anymore. My mom, my friends and their moms, and some people at school knew. I felt ashamed. But I really needed the support, so it was good that they knew and could help me.

I sometimes felt like the whole world knew my secret that wasn't a secret anymore. I felt like everyone was looking at me. I wished no one could see me. I prayed that I would just disappear one day and it would be all over.

Even though I went to school most days, I didn't say much in classes because I didn't want to draw attention to myself. I didn't know what to say to people, even my friends. Should I talk about what was constantly nagging at my thoughts—Dad and the trial? Or, should I talk about boys and sports and music and classes, and pretend that everything was cool—like I did before? It was hard, I didn't know what to do, how to be, where to start.

It helped a lot when my friends would come up to me and start conversations. Like at lunch one day, Joy came over and said, "Hey, Janie. So what do you think about that substitute teacher in history class? What a bore!" Joy broke the ice and just acted natural to me. I felt drawn into the conversation. I remember smiling that day. I didn't feel so isolated or weird.

I was pretty nervous a lot, and jumpy. One day at school the hall was kind of empty and I was getting a notebook from my locker. This guy, Dan, who I kind of liked, called to me from down the hall. "Hi, Jane!" He startled me, for sure, and I dropped all my books on my foot. I felt so scared and stupid for dropping everything, I started to cry. Dan said he was "so sorry" for scaring me, and he helped me pick up all my stuff. I don't remember exactly what he said next, but somehow he got me laughing. Crying and laughing, sometimes they happen together.

That afternoon, Dan and I went out for some fries and a Coke. I had fun. We didn't talk about my real life, my dad, I mean. We talked about school and books and movies. I laughed. It felt so good.

As things about the abuse and the trial became public, more people found out. And not all the kids were as nice to me as Joy and Dan. Some were totally cruel, and I hated them. Some days I thought I'd never go back to school. Some days I was going to leave town, change my name and start a whole new life. Cathy helped me through a lot of tears and hate about those kids. It's times of trouble like this that you find out who your true friends are.

I was beginning to learn about trust. I had been pretty mixed up about that.

Section 14

The Indictment

It had been an uneventful day. I was beginning to feel a little calmer, and didn't even jump when the phone rang at home late that afternoon. It was Nina Santiago calling to tell me that the grand jury had handed down an indictment against my father. She said he would be sent a **summons** to appear in superior court for **arraignment** within the next few days. My hand felt frozen to the phone. My thoughts were whirling.

I knew that Andrea had explained arraignment to me, but I guess I forgot. I stammered as I asked Nina, "What's arraignment?"

She explained. "Arraignment is the public reading in the court of the formal charges against your father. Because of the indictment from the grand jury, your father will receive a summons in the mail which will tell him when to report to court. At the arraignment in court, the charges filed against him will be read to him, and he will **plead** "guilty" or "not guilty." Just so you know, Jane, it is pretty standard for all defendants charged with serious crimes to plead "not guilty" at the time of arraignment. This has nothing to do with whether or not they plead guilty later in the process. Jane? Jane, are you there?"

I was there, but I had drifted off into the frenzy of my whirling thoughts. Was this all really happening?

"Oh, by the way, Jane," Nina continued, "Remember we mentioned that although it's not very common, sometimes indictments handed down by the grand jury might appear in the local newspapers. Your name won't be mentioned in the papers because the law says the media cannot use your name. However, your father's name and address might be in the papers."

"Oh no." I thought. "Now everyone will know." I hid my face in my hands and cried.

Section 15

The Arraignment

Life was in slow motion for me, but the day finally came. Mom and I didn't go to the arraignment. It was a really "quick procedure" Nina said, so she was the only one who needed to be there. She said it was important for my father to understand that the charges were being brought against him by the Commonwealth of Massachusetts, not by me or my mom. That fact would be clearer to him if we weren't there for the arraignment. But I might as well have been there. I couldn't think of anything else all day. I imagined the scene over and over in my mind. I was grateful that Dad wouldn't have to be handcuffed. Some of the defendants being arraigned are handcuffed, you know.

Nina finally called late in the day. I stayed home from school, waiting to hear from her. Believe me, it was a very long day. "As expected," Nina said, "Your dad pled 'not guilty.' There was a **bail hearing,** and **bail** was set so he won't have to be in jail." I was glad. Nina said that court dates had been set for **pretrial conferences** and **motions hearings**. But I didn't have to go to them. "The actual trial date," she said, "could be scheduled anytime from three months to one year from now."

I screeched. I know I screeched, "A year!" I was totally shocked.

Nina said, "Jane, it might even be longer. Sometimes there are **continuances** in court that we can't control. Realistically, though, the trial could happen in September or October." This was December. September, October. That seemed like never.

I called Andrea later after I had calmed down. "What's a continuance?" I asked.

And she told me. "A continuance is a change in the date that something is scheduled to happen in court."

Now I had more questions! "Why does that happen? Will it happen to me?"

She answered, "It happens because of lots of different reasons. Sometimes the lawyers need to do more research on the legal issues. Sometimes a witness is not available. Sometimes a previously scheduled trial takes longer than expected, so the judge is busy with that and not ready for us. I don't know if any continuances will happen for your case, Jane, but it's probable, so be prepared." She also said that most likely Mom and I would be notified in advance about any delays or changes. When it was time for the trial we would receive **subpoenas** telling us when to appear in court. "By then," Andrea said, "things should be pretty well set and ready to go."

Section 16

Waiting Again

I could not believe that it took so long for a trial to be held in superior court. It's about "scheduling" they told me, and lots of cases for the judges to hear. It was hard for me because there was nothing I could do about it but wait. Sometimes I was frantic, but mostly there was just nothing anyone could do about it.

Eventually I settled down into a routine, and a routine felt nice for a change. I still called Andrea a lot, and she called me regularly to check in about how I was doing and to keep me informed about the progress of my case. I saw Cathy every week, and I really started to like her and trust her, too. But sometimes I wasn't sure why I went. I didn't really want to talk about the abuse. Sometimes I just wanted to forget the whole thing.

The house was quieter. Mom seemed to calm down some, too, but there was definitely an empty spot without Dad. He didn't bother us by calling much anymore. Weeks earlier, Nina had filed for a **restraining order** to keep him from seeing me or contacting me. Dad called Mom at her job if he needed to talk to her about something.

Sometimes Mom and I could put our troubles aside. "File them for future reference," Cathy would say. And during those times we had some fun together.

The holidays that year were very strange.

Section 17

The Empty Courtroom

Although Mom and I went on with our regular lives, we both felt like there was this gray storm cloud hovering above us all the time. It followed us. I wondered if Dad had one, too.

In early July, Andrea called to tell me that a trial date had been set for August 18. I shivered, and it was 90 degrees outside! She did remind me, however, that things could come up to cause delays.

During the last week in July and the first week in August, Nina, Andrea, and I met a few times to go over what would happen in court. First they talked to me about the verdict. Andrea said, "We know your Dad is guilty, Jane. But during the trial, we need to prove his guilt, beyond a reasonable doubt. Remember? We talked about reasonable doubt."

I nodded.

Andrea was being very serious. She continued talking. "In cases like this, sometimes the **defendant** is found **not guilty.** If that happens, Jane, it doesn't mean that your dad is innocent, or that he didn't abuse you. It means that the district attorney's office did not have sufficient evidence to convince the jury of his guilt beyond a reasonable doubt." Andrea told me this to "prepare me," she said, for the possibility that my dad might be **acquitted** rather than **convicted.** I knew it was a possibility, but I told Andrea that I didn't want to even think about it.

One afternoon Andrea and Nina took me to an empty courtroom so I wouldn't be going into a totally strange place when the trial started. We went into the courtroom. It looked dark and somber, and it felt cold. In fact, a shiver went up my back as I stood in the doorway and looked around. I knew right away this was a very serious place.

Nina coaxed me into sitting in the **witness stand.** As she and Andrea looked through some papers to decide on the questions I would be asked, I just sat and looked around, slowly. I had to remind myself to breathe. I felt hot tears burning my eyes. I squeezed my eyes shut really tight, hoping the tears would go away, hoping when I opened my eyes I would be away. In Florida maybe, at Disney World, in Hawaii, or maybe Spain. I've always wanted to go to Spain. My hands actually gripped the arms of the chair. I was hoping with all my might.

And then I heard Andrea's voice. "Jane. Jane, what's happening?"

I opened my eyes and was surprised to see her, and Nina and the empty courtroom. It didn't look so scary now because it wasn't the first time I was seeing it. It actually looked familiar. "I'm OK," I said.

So while I was sitting there, supposedly "getting comfortable," Nina spent some time preparing for what might come up in the trial. I knew this was going to be hard.

Then Andrea helped me step down from the stand. I was a little shaky, but I felt very mature and grown-up.

Section 18

Pretrial Details

A lot of paperwork goes into a trial. I learned that first thing. Before the trial actually happens, the ADA and the **defense attorney** meet in court with the **judge** and the court workers (the **court officers,** the **judge's clerk,** and the **court reporters**), to submit and decide about the **pretrial motions.** That's when the attorneys request certain procedures and special conditions. For example, Nina asked for a microphone to use during my testimony. She knew I talked softly, especially when we got to the parts that were hard for me to say. She wanted to make sure the judge, the jury, and everyone could hear me. The defense attorney didn't want Nina to refer to me as a **victim,** but to call me a **complaining witness** instead. Andrea explained that this was because the word victim implied that I was hurt by my dad, and that's what the ADA had to prove. "It's a technicality," she said. The judge decided to "wait and see" about the microphone, but I wish he hadn't done that. He said I had to be referred to as a complaining witness. The court process—the whole thing—was hard for me. Sometimes I didn't understand, and I really wondered whose side they were on.

Section 19

Delays and Preparations

And there were continuances. I'm glad Nina and Andrea warned me about them, but even their warnings didn't help my stress about it. We'd be all ready for the trial to start the next week, and Andrea or Nina would call to say it had to be rescheduled for later.

It happened a few times, and each time I got mad at Andrea or Nina, whichever one called to tell me the news. But then I felt bad about being mad at them. They were really nice to me, and on my side. I knew that. After all, the judge was the person who was in charge of the courtroom, and the delays were mostly for administrative reasons. But I could never figure out how those things, whatever they were, could be more important than people's feelings. I was very upset about all this waiting and delaying, and so was my mom. I wondered if they cared about us at all. I had waited so long already, and I didn't know if I could stand waiting one minute longer. Mom called my upset "apprehension." Fear of future evil! That felt like an accurate description. But in spite of all the distress, I somehow made it through the waiting.

For months before the trial I spent most of my free time preparing myself by watching lawyer shows on television. I almost never missed *Judge Judy* or *Law and Order* or *The Practice*. And sometimes I'd stay up late and watch reruns of the original *Perry Mason*. I prayed that Nina was a better prosecutor than poor Mr. Burger!

I was fascinated, yet frightened by this television law. Even though Andrea talked to me a lot about the legal process and the language that would be used in court, I thought I could become some kind of "expert" from my TV research, and then I'd be less afraid. Andrea and Nina had both talked to me about television law, warning me that some of it was "realistic" and some of it was "just drama" geared to entertain TV audiences. But I watched the shows anyway.

Unfortunately those TV shows didn't help me to feel more confident when my real day in court finally came. But they did keep me occupied during the long months of waiting. Watching them helped me feel like I was doing something to prepare myself.

Section 20

The Trial Begins

The trial was finally scheduled to begin on October 4. "A firm date," Nina said. Mom and I had received subpoenas in the mail requesting our appearance as witnesses for the prosecution in the case of *The Commonwealth of Massachusetts vs. My Dad.* The documents had a serious, cold look about them, just like the courtroom.

The trial did start on October 4. It lasted for five days from the jury **empaneling** to the reading of the **verdict.** These were by far, the longest, yet the quickest, five days of my entire life. When the trial was in progress, even the minutes crawled by. The days seemed endless. And the sleepless nights were frightfully endless. But when the trial was all over, it seemed to have lasted no longer than the blink of an eye.

Section 21

In Court

Court was a tense place. It was very organized, and the people who worked there seemed to know exactly what was going on. But in spite of knowing, even they seemed tense.

There were a lot of people in court. There were two lawyers (Nina and Mr. McCarthy, who was the defense attorney for my dad). There were two court officers. They had on uniforms sort of like police officers. There was a court clerk who sat at a desk in front of the judge's bench, and a court reporter who recorded every word of the trial. I was surprised that there were fourteen people on the jury instead of twelve. I kept counting them, thinking I made a mistake. When I asked Andrea, she explained that two jurors were alternates in case someone on the jury got sick or something. There were also a few people in the audience. Most trials are open to the public. I wanted to know who the people were and why they were there. I was upset to see my grandparents and Uncle John sitting behind my dad. They didn't believe me, and at the trial they didn't even look at me. I just knew they hated me, and I was sad and upset and I didn't want them to be there.

I appreciated Andrea more as each minute passed. She stayed with me the whole time. I didn't realize it, but because my mom was also a witness, we couldn't always be together in the courtroom. There's this thing called **sequestered.** It means that one witness is not allowed to hear the testimony of the other witnesses, so as not to be influence by what someone else says. So I had to spend a lot of time with Andrea in the victim/witness "waiting" room (what a perfect name for that room), wondering what in the world was going on inside the courtroom. There was this huge clock on the wall in the waiting room, and I just stared at it, watching the endless seconds tick by. At first I asked Andrea a lot of questions because I was so nervous.

But then I drifted off into my worries. Mom was getting divorced. Dad might go to jail. And I was going to have to say totally embarrassing things in the courtroom.

Mom and I were in court on the third, fourth, and fifth days of the trial. We didn't have to be there for the jury selection or the pretrial motions that happened during the first two days.

First Nina and Mr. McCarthy gave their **opening statements.** That part was sort of like the TV shows. Then Nina called me to the witness stand to testify. I was so nervous my hands were sweaty. My stomach was upset, and I was afraid I would throw up. But I didn't. It was hard to testify, for sure. But I did it. I was OK.

Nina stood across the courtroom and asked me questions. The easy ones were first. My name, address, age, school . . . and then came the hard ones. Nina began to ask me questions about the sexual experiences I had with my dad. "Oh no," I thought, "I can't say this!" Nina kept asking me to speak up, but I could barely speak at all.

Then all of a sudden, the judge jumped up from his chair. His unexpected movement, right in the middle of my testimony, scared me. He abruptly said, "We're in **recess.** Counsel, in my chambers." Surrounded by a cloud of swirling black fabric, the judge disappeared from the courtroom, followed by the lawyers.

I started to cry. I couldn't figure out what was happening. Before I knew it, I was out in the corridor and Andrea was right beside me. I got some water, and Andrea tried to calm me down. A few minutes later, the court officers were installing a microphone on the witness stand for me to use. Nina came out into the corridor and explained that the judge couldn't hear my answers and asked that the microphone be set up. I wished that the judge had approved Nina's pretrial motion for a microphone in the first place, because now I was upset and feeling afraid of him.

Fifteen minutes later court was back in session. The judge spoke to me directly and apologized for the disruption. He asked me to speak clearly into the microphone "so the jury can hear every word." I think he smiled at me. I know I didn't smile. I just nodded.

Section 22

Cross-Examination

When Nina finished asking me questions, Dad's lawyer, Mr. Mc-Carthy, **cross-examined** me. He was loud and abrupt. At times I felt attacked by him. He tried to confuse me by asking me the same question over in different ways. Later Andrea explained that he was trying to "discredit" my testimony.

Mr. McCarthy's confusing questions made it hard for me to think. I felt those now familiar tears stinging my eyes. My fists were clenched in my lap. I wanted to run out of the courtroom, and not stop running until I got to Spain. But then I would see Andrea—she was like an anchor for me—and I somehow found the strength to sit still and go on.

I answered the questions in the best way I could. But Mr. McCarthy kept saying he didn't understand. So he'd ask the same question again, and again. Finally, the judge interrupted. He rephrased Mr. Mc-Carthy's last question, which had been asked several times, and my answer. He then looked directly at me and asked, "Is this what you're saying, Jane?"

"Yes," I said as I nodded.

The judge turned to Dad's lawyer and said, "Well, then. That's quite enough for this question, Mr. McCarthy. I think that both the jury and I understand the witness's answer. Please move on."

I felt such relief, I can't even say. The judge's interruption helped me calm down, and Mr. McCarthy didn't seem so mean from then on. But still, I was exceedingly glad when it was finally over. I was questioned for almost three hours total.

That afternoon and part of the next day there were other witnesses. My mom, Cathy, and my doctor also testified. After that, my dad testified even though his lawyer didn't want him to, and he didn't have to. Andrea explained that Dad didn't have to testify because of the **Fifth Amendment,** and because the **burden of proof** is on the prosecution. My Uncle John testified for my dad as a **character witness.** I didn't hear any of the testimony because I was sequestered.

At the end of the examination of witnesses, both lawyers gave their **closing arguments** to the court. I was there for that. Hearing Mr. McCarthy speak was very scary. He said that he was completely convinced my dad was not guilty. He said that I was mistaken. "Children misunderstand and misinterpret." He said that I lied. "Children have vivid imaginations, and they sometimes fabricate dramatic tales to get attention." That's what Mr. McCarthy had to say about me.

But then Nina's closing argument restored my faith and confidence. She said I didn't lie, and that I wasn't mistaken.

I felt like I was on a roller coaster. I wondered how the jury felt.

Section 23

Instructions to the Jury

After the closing arguments, the judge spoke directly to the jury for what seemed like a very long time. I wondered how in the world they could ever remember everything he said.

The judge told the jury to weigh the **credibility** of the witnesses, and to decide whether to believe some, none, or all of what each person said. I thought it must be very hard to be a juror. I mean, I said my dad had sex with me, and he said he didn't. How does the jury decide who's telling the truth and who's telling a lie?

The judge went on to further instruct the jury. He reminded them that my dad was **"presumed innocent."** I shivered when I heard those words. The judge said that the prosecution must prove guilt beyond a "reasonable doubt," but not *all* doubt. I started thinking that must be where the old saying came from, the one about giving someone the "benefit of the doubt."

Then the judge went over the elements of the charges against my dad for the jury to hear, reminding them that Dad was charged with rape of a child. Then the judge read these things called **statutes.** "Whoever has sexual intercourse or unnatural sexual intercourse . . . abuses a child under the age of sixteen." It all sounded so impersonal, I couldn't believe he was still talking about me. The jury was then told that they had two choices for a verdict: not guilty or guilty as charged.

When the judge finished talking to the jury, the court clerk took this wooden box and shook it up. It looked like he was going to draw the winning name for a raffle. I was kind of startled by this familiar, friendly action that seemed so out of place. The clerk drew two names from the box, but instead of winning something, the names identified the alternate jurors. The other twelve jurors left the courtroom and went into the jury room to **deliberate.**

"All rise." The judge swiftly left the courtroom followed by his fluttering black robes. The trial was suddenly over.

I turned to Andrea with hope in my eyes and a question in my voice. "It's over?"

"Not yet, Jane," she replied. "It's not over yet."

Section 24

The Verdict

Nina suggested that Mom and I go to the cafeteria for lunch. She said we shouldn't go home or leave the courthouse. She wanted us to be close as we waited for the verdict. We went to the cafeteria and ate lunch, and then spent the rest of the afternoon waiting with Andrea in the victim/witness waiting room. I swear, I have every detail of that room memorized!

At 3:30 p.m. Nina appeared in the doorway of the waiting room. The jury had reached a verdict.

And then we were back in the courtroom. I have never in my life been so scared. Andrea stayed right beside me the whole time. This was a totally terrible situation. I was feeling panicky because I wasn't sure what I wanted the verdict to be. If it was "guilty" then maybe my dad would go to jail, or at least he would be in a lot of trouble. He'd have a criminal record. But even worse, if the verdict was "not guilty" probably everyone would think I was a liar. I had this terrible headache. My teeth were clenched so tight. My fists were, too. Andrea kept trying to get me to be more relaxed, but there was absolutely no possibility of relaxed!

The jury filed in. The judge appeared. "All rise." I was becoming accustomed to the routine. "This court is now in session." What followed felt like a dream or a movie. Something unreal, anyway. In fact, if I think about it, I can still play back the entire scene in my mind just as if I were seeing it happen all over again.

The judge spoke. "Men and women of the jury, have you reached a verdict?"

The foreman stood and replied. "We have, your honor." The clerk asked my dad to stand, and he did. So did his lawyer. And then the verdict. **"Guilty as charged."** Guilty as charged . . . guilty as charged. An echo. I'm sure I heard an echo in the cold, hollow courtroom.

Movement and sound happened slowly and distinctly. I couldn't see my father's face, but when the guilty verdict was announced, his whole body slumped forward, looking defeated. My face and hands finally relaxed. Dad sat down and held his head in his hands. Was he crying? I was. My tears were a release of tension mixed with feelings of great loss. Would I ever have a dad again?

The judge spoke. His voice startled me. "The jury is dismissed. The court thanks you for your service. Sentencing will be in two weeks. This court is adjourned." And in that now familiar flurry of swirling black, the judge was gone.

Section 25

After the Trial

In slow motion I turned to Andrea. I looked up at her and very softly asked, "It's over now?"

"Well, not quite, Jane," she answered. "The trial is over, but the court process is not. At the sentencing hearing, in two weeks, the judge will hear sentence recommendations from both Nina and Mr. McCarthy. And if you want to say something, there will also be time for you to make a **victim impact statement.** Or, you can write a letter to the judge telling him how you feel about your dad's sentence. In fact, sometimes before the sentencing people write to the judge about the defendant, and you need to be prepared for that. Your father may have character witnesses—like your grandparents and your uncle, or your dad's boss, or his minister—who write on his behalf, suggesting that he receive **probation** and not be sentenced to jail at all, or that he receive a short sentence."

I just nodded in response, and Andrea continued. "Nina will discuss her sentencing recommendations with you directly before she says anything to the judge. I know that you've thought a lot about what kind of sentence you want your dad to receive, Jane. And now is the time for you to decide if you want to make a victim impact statement. You can either say your statement in court the day of the sentencing, or you can write it to the judge. We encourage you to communicate your feelings to the court in some way, so your voice will be heard, but you don't have to. You don't have to say anything. You don't have to write anything. You don't even have to go to the sentencing hearing."

Andrea and I had similar talks before, but hearing it all again left me in a daze. Maybe I was dazed because I thought it was over. I hoped it was over. I wanted it over. Two more weeks seemed like another eternity, but I knew I'd get through it somehow. I mean, really! Look at what I'd been through already!

During the next several days, I spent my time after school alone, going for long walks, mostly. Thinking. It was fall and it felt good to be outside in the bright, crisp sunshine. I walked and walked, trying very hard to get to the bottom of my feelings about Dad. Talking with Cathy helped, but I knew that identifying my own feelings was really a solitary activity. And so I walked some more. Finally, after ten days I sat down very late at night and wrote the victim impact statement I would read in the courtroom.

My statement was short. I thought that was best. I honestly didn't know how much I would be able to say without crying.

Section 26

Victim Impact Statement

Since I'm only sixteen years old, I can't know for sure, but I think that writing this statement, and then saying it out loud in court, may be the hardest thing I will ever do in my whole life.

In spite of everything my dad has done to me, including the actual abuse and that he said I lied about it, and in spite of how bad I feel sometimes, both physically and emotionally, I still love my dad very much. And I know he loves me.

But he hurt me. He scared me and threatened me. He confused me. My own father stole things from me, important things, that I can never, ever recover. My body was violated. My heart is broken, and I think my spirit is too. My family is shattered. We have all suffered so much. Nobody should have to go through this.

Dad did something wrong, something very wrong and bad. He always punishes me when I'm bad. It seems only fair that he should be punished now. I love my dad, and feel very bad about the idea of him being in jail. But I don't want him to hurt me anymore. I want to feel safe. If he's in jail, and can't see me or call me, then, maybe, for the first time in my life, I can feel safe.

I also want my dad to see a doctor or therapist who can help him. So then maybe he won't hurt other people like he hurt Mom and me.

Section 27

Sentencing

The day of the sentencing hearing finally arrived. Mom and Andrea and I were sitting in the courtroom at exactly 2:00 p.m., the time the hearing was scheduled. Except for Nina and the court officers, the room was empty. I was nervous and confused. At five minutes past 2:00, more people started coming, but I didn't know who they were. In and out. People kept coming in and going out of the courtroom.

I whispered to Andrea a question I had asked her several times before. "What kind of sentence will Dad get?"

"Well," she whispered in reply, "there are guidelines regarding appropriate sentencing for every crime, but the decision in each case is really up to the judge."

At ten minutes past 2:00, more people came in. "Who are all these people?" I asked Andrea.

Other activities were scheduled in court that afternoon. They were lawyers and victim witness advocates and witnesses and friends. Some were Dad's friends. I noticed that the lawyers seemed friendly to each other, even if they were on opposite sides. When Mr. McCarthy arrived, Nina shook his hand and spoke to him. I didn't want them to be friendly.

At 2:15, I started going in and out of the courtroom. Getting a drink, going to the bathroom. This waiting made me so nervous. Andrea told me that sometimes the waiting is the worst part. I thought maybe she was right. At 2:20, the court officer started talking on the telephone on his desk and this one lawyer over in the corner was throwing his pen up in the air catching it each time it came down again. Was he nervous, too? Or just passing the time? It seemed to me that nothing at court ever started on time. I don't know why, either, but it made me very nervous. I wondered if whoever was in charge had any idea about how nerve-racking all this waiting was. My heart was pounding so hard, that I worried I might be having a heart attack. But I wasn't.

Finally people slowly began taking their places. They sat down and one by one became quiet. Dad came in and sat on the other side of the courtroom. He didn't even look at me.

"All rise." The judge appeared. "Be seated. This court is now in session." A solemn quiet. The clerk announced the other cases, stated who was present, and who the lawyers were. Now things seemed to happen very quickly, and soon the courtroom was nearly empty.

The clerk announced our case and acknowledged Nina and Mr. McCarthy as the lawyers. Dad went forward and sat next to Mr. McCarthy.

Then Nina stood. I stopped breathing, I think. Nina spoke directly to the judge. Her voice was clear and loud. It echoed in the hollow, quiet space. "Thank you, Your Honor. On behalf of the commonwealth, the district attorney's office recommends a state prison sentence. The sexual abuse of a dependent child is the most heinous of crimes. Jane's father made her childhood into a living nightmare. She was a helpless, defenseless, loving child. A father is supposed to protect and care for his child, not molest her. Jane suffered the ultimate betrayal by her own father, and nothing we do here today can heal her wounds. However, what we can do is hold her father responsible for his crimes. This young girl endured over ten years of abuse. There is physical evidence and psychological damage. Her father was found guilty by a jury of his peers. Although we cannot take away Jane's suffering, we can send a message to other child molesters, through this molester, that our society will not tolerate the mistreatment of our children. Therefore, the commonwealth recommends a state prison sentence, to be followed by a **suspended sentence** from and after the committed sentence, during which time sex offender counseling will be mandatory."

When Nina was finished, it was my turn to speak. I walked up to the witness stand and sat down. I was feeling kind of shaky. I unfolded my paper and looked at Nina and then at the judge. I looked at Dad. I wanted him to look at me, but he was staring at his hands which were fiddling with some papers on the table in front if him. I read my statement, grateful that it was short, because I did start to cry. This whole situation was a terrible nightmare. I still couldn't believe it was happening. I felt so sad, so bad about it all. Why did you do this, Dad?

I finished my statement, folded up my paper, and went back to my place next to Andrea. I was glad the court officer was there to help me step down from the stand.

Then Mr. McCarthy spoke on my dad's behalf. "He is not a one-dimensional person. He is a son, a husband, a father. We cannot deny him his humanity. He has provided for his family responsibly. The judge has received a number of letters from friends and relatives who have known him for more than twenty years. He has a friendly, generous spirit . . . " Mr. McCarthy went on and on saying what a great man my dad was. It was hard for me to believe that Nina and Mr. McCarthy were talking about the same person.

And then the judge talked, for a long time it seemed, before getting to the point. He asked Dad to stand. Then the clerk announced the sentence. "You have been found guilty . . . you are sentenced to a state prison term . . . to be followed by a suspended sentence . . . will include mandatory counseling . . . sentence to begin immediately." The court officers came up to Dad and led him away through the mysterious door in the back of the courtroom.

Time stopped for me. Shocked, stunned. I don't know. A shiver went through my whole body. People were talking to me. I saw their mouths move, but didn't hear their voices. Andrea sort of steered me out of the courtroom and into the victim/witness waiting room. I sat down, and burst into tears.

Well, the trial was finally over. But now the part about putting my life back together was about to begin.

Section 28

Toward Recovery

It hasn't been quite two years since I first told Mrs. Winston about the sexual abuse, but it seems like it all happened centuries ago. Since the trial ended I've felt that I can get on with my life. No, that's not quite right. I feel that I'm finally beginning to live my life.

In some ways I feel lucky. Not lucky that my dad abused me, that wasn't lucky at all. That was frightening and destructive. But, I feel lucky that there are people who care about kids, and that some of those people helped me. In fact, they're still helping me. I see Cathy every week, and probably will keep seeing her for awhile. She's helped me to understand the experience of incest and to work on my feelings about it. Sorting out my feelings can be very, very hard work, and will "take some time," Cathy said. I mostly hate thinking about it and getting upset about it, but then the upset and work seem worthwhile when I finally come to understand more about my experience and to accept it.

I feel sad every time I think about my dad. I probably always will feel sad about him. I'm really angry at him, too. But even though I feel sad and angry about the abuse and what Dad did to our family, I still love him. I can't help it. After all, he's my dad.

He's in jail now. I don't visit him or write to him. I'm still too upset. But Cathy thinks maybe someday I'll want to tell him how hurt and angry I am. I sure hope he learns something while he's in jail. I hope he understands how much he hurt me and that what he did to me was wrong, and that he can never sexually abuse a child ever again. He wants me to forgive him, and I said I would think about it. But I'm not sure I can forgive him. I need to be 100 percent sure he's truly sorry, so sorry that he will never even consider abusing another child.

Given the life I've survived so far, things are going as well as can be expected. I'm doing okay in school. My grades aren't bad, and last spring I even got up the courage to try out for the track team. I made

Varsity! I've dated a little, very little, but enough to realize that I have a lot to learn about relationships and sex. "But doesn't everyone!" Cathy said.

Sometimes it's tempting to think about burying my past and my pain with drugs and alcohol, like some kids at school do. But I resist. I know that keeping things buried won't help much in the long run. Sometimes I have nightmares. Sometimes I'm tired and sick with headaches and stomachaches. Sometimes life isn't very fun for me. But now I at least feel like I'm living it, and that I'm in control of my own body and my own life. I really like that feeling. For the first time in my whole life I'm feeling and expressing, and being "me"! I've discovered that "me" is happy and sad and angry and confused and hopeful and discouraged and frightened and courageous and . . .

In a way, I'm sorry I can't end this story by telling you that I "lived happily ever after." But I'm only sixteen years old, so this isn't anywhere near the end. Anyway, that happily ever after stuff is for kids and fairy tales. This is real life, my life. Oh, I'll never forget what my father did, and I'll never forget the pain. But I'm going to keep working at understanding myself and what happened, because I firmly believe that with work and persistence, life will be better. I have lots of hope for the future thanks to Mrs. Winston and Patty O'Neill and Andrea and Nina and Cathy and Mom and . . . well, you know, thanks to everyone who helped me and everyone who cared.

Guiding Questions

Section 1. *I'm Jane*

1. Do you remember how old you were when the abuse you experienced started?
2. When and how did you realize that what was happening to you was abuse?
3. What feelings and reactions did you experience while the abuse was happening?
4. As a result of her abuse, Jane felt confusion, fear, anxiety, upset, and physical illness. But she pretended that everything was fine. Were your reactions similar to Jane's? Did you experience other feelings and reactions as well?

Section 2. *The First Time I Told*

1. How did you decide to tell someone about the abuse?
2. Who did you first tell about the abuse? What was helpful about his or her reaction?
3. After she told Mrs. Winston about the abuse, Jane felt a mixture of feelings: relief, gratitude, guilt, fear, shame. These are *some* of the feelings teens experience after disclosing abuse. What feelings did you experience after you told?
4. Did the person you told notify anyone else? If so, how did/do you feel about other people knowing?
5. Did you know that your state had a Mandated Reporter Law regarding child abuse?

Section 3. *Making a Report*

1. How did/do you feel about your abuse being reported to the social service and legal authorities?
2. Jane's guidance counselor gave her a telephone number for a twenty-four-hour crisis line. How do you think that calling the

crisis line would have helped Jane? How do you think it would help you to call a crisis line?

3. After Jane's disclosure, her feelings became very intense. She tried to manage her feelings by retreating to her room, listening to music, watching TV, pacing, and hurting herself by twisting her fingers. What do you do to help manage intense feelings?

Section 4. The Investigation Begins

1. When the legal investigation began, it was difficult for Jane to wait for the various steps in the process to happen. How do you react to having to wait? How do you react to not knowing what the outcome of your situation will be? How do you calm and comfort yourself during the necessary times of waiting and not knowing?

2. If you felt afraid during the disclosure and investigation, were you also able to feel brave for doing the right thing and telling someone about the abuse?

3. Why do you think that the person who abused you did it?

Section 5. I'm Sorry, Mom

1. Sometimes a parent can be supportive and helpful to an abused teen, as Jane's mom was. Sometimes parents and other family members are too upset about the abuse and too worried about what will happen to be supportive of the teen. What was it like for you when your family first learned about the abuse?

2. How do you feel about the idea of going to counseling? How do you think it will help you to talk with someone about the abuse that happened to you?

3. How did/do you feel about telling more people about the abuse?

4. How did/do you think that your friends and relatives and teachers and other people you know will feel about you after they find out about the abuse?

5. Jane did not want to have to tell more people about the abuse, but her mom said "Yes" to the interview in order to protect Jane. How do you feel about taking steps to stop your abuser?

Section 6. The Interview

1. What were some of the feelings you experienced before, during, and after your interview?
2. How did/do you feel about saying exactly what happened to you?
3. Jane felt ashamed and guilty saying words such as penis and vagina. What words are hard for you to say?
4. Jane felt proud of herself for being strong enough to do something that was so scary. How do you feel about yourself when you do something that is very hard for you to do?

Section 7. After the Interview

1. The investigation and prosecution processes were confusing to Jane because they were all new and different. If the processes seem confusing to you or your family, what can you do to help yourself better understand what is happening?
2. What do you want to happen to your abuser if he or she is found guilty?
3. How will you feel if your abuser is found not guilty?
4. How do you feel about not knowing what the outcome of the case will be?
5. How do you feel about the possibility of your abuser being arrested?
6. What opinions do you and members of your family have about counseling?

Section 8. Counseling

1. How did you feel (physically and emotionally) before you told people about the abuse? How did you feel after you told?
2. Do you think you would call a therapist or a crisis line if you wanted or needed to talk with someone? Why? Why not?
3. Jane made a list of items to talk about with her therapist, Cathy. How do you feel about the items on Jane's list? How is your list the same and different? Write a list of items you want to talk about or know more about.

Section 9. Prosecution Begins

1. Sometimes it is not a good idea for a victim of child sexual abuse to go forward with prosecution. How will you know if it is a good idea for you to go forward?
2. What do you think about the concept that someone accused of a crime is considered innocent until proven guilty?
3. What are some of the words or practices in the criminal justice system that you find confusing?

Section 10. Pretrial Testimony

1. How has the fact of your abuse affected other members of your family?
2. How was the interview handled in your case? How did/do you feel about this process?
3. What was/is the hardest thing for you to talk about regarding the abuse?
4. What helps you trust that you can count on people to be there for you?

Section 11. Counseling Support

1. How were/are you feeling about your abuser after your disclosure and during the investigation process?
2. Who can you talk with about any feelings you have that are difficult for you or that you do not understand?
3. How do you feel about having the power to stop the prosecution at any time?

Section 12. Waiting

1. What information do you need to help you better understand why the court process takes so long?
2. Waiting is difficult for most people. How do you cope with waiting?

Section 13. At School

1. What kind of support do you need at school? How can you ask for what you need?

2. How did people in your life (friends, family, teachers) react when they learned that you had been sexually abused? Which reactions were helpful? Which ones hurt you? Why?
3. How do you know whom to trust?

Section 14. The Indictment

1. How do you feel about the possibility that your abuser's name will appear in the newspaper and on television?
2. What do the laws in your state say about keeping the victim's name private? (*Note:* You can check with your state legislator's office for this information or ask your victim witness advocate.)

Section 15. The Arraignment

1. How do you feel about the amount of time your case is taking?
2. Do you understand the reasons for any delays? What are they?
3. What kind of support do you need to help you through this long process?
4. Are there any words in this chapter that you don't understand? (*Note:* The vocabulary used in court and about the court process is unique. Consult the **glossary** and ask questions anytime you do not understand a word.)

Section 16. Waiting Again

1. How do you feel about the possibility of your abuser contacting you or trying to see you?
2. If you feel afraid of your abuser, what steps have been taken to keep you safe?
3. If you think it's a good idea to put your troubles aside sometimes, how do you do that?

Section 17. The Empty Courtroom

1. What do you think it means to prove the defendant's guilt beyond a reasonable doubt?
2. How will you feel if your abuser is acquitted (found not guilty) by the jury? How will you feel if your abuser is convicted (found guilty)?

3. Do you think it is a good idea to visit the empty courtroom before the trial? Would you like to do this? Why? Why not?

Section 18. Pretrial Details

1. Sometimes judges will make minor accommodations for young victims and witnesses. Sometimes they will not make accommodations. But, it is important to ask for whatever you need to help make the process less stressful for you. What kind of accommodations do you think will be helpful to you in court? Why? Have you discussed accommodations with your victim witness advocate? Have you asked what accommodations in the courtroom have been allowed on other cases and helpful to other kids?
2. When Jane got upset about the court process, she wondered, "Whose side are they on?" Sometimes abuse victims feel revictimized by the court process. How do you feel about how your case is being handled?

Section 19. Delays and Preparations

1. How do you feel when you are informed about delays in the trial date?
2. There will be months of waiting before the trial begins. What can you do while you are waiting for the trial to start to help yourself feel prepared?

Section 20. The Trial Begins

1. How did/do you feel about the trial finally starting?
2. The experience of being in court will be different for each victim and witness. What was/is the trial like for you? What part of the experience surprised you the most? What part did/do you dislike the most?

Section 21. In Court

1. The courtroom is a tense place, and the beginning of a trial sparks intense emotions. What feelings do/did you have as you anticipate(d) the trial?
2. Were there parts of the trial that you did not understand or that you found particularly upsetting? (For example, the number of

jurors, or the sequestering of witnesses, or the court being open to the public.) Who can you ask to help you better understand the process and/or to support you through upsetting experiences?

3. Testifying before open court is stressful for everyone—even adults. How can you be prepared for this stress, and how can you take good care of yourself after testifying?

4. Did any unusual circumstances or events take place during your trial? How did you cope with these?

Section 22. Cross-Examination

1. The purpose of cross-examination is to cast doubt on the witness' testimony. This can be confusing and upsetting. What do you think will be the hardest part about being cross-examined? What can you do to be prepared?

2. How will you feel if the defense attorney says that you imagined the abuse or lied about the abuse? What kind of support do you need to deal with this possibility? Would it be better for you to not hear the closing arguments? Why?

Section 23. Instructions to the Jury

1. How do you determine if someone is telling the truth or lying?

2. How do you think members of a jury go about determining who is telling the truth and who is lying?

Section 24. The Verdict

1. Even after going through the investigation and the trial, Jane was not sure about what she wanted the verdict to be. How do you feel about the verdict your abuser received?

2. Are you surprised at all by your feelings? Why? Why not?

Section 25. After the Trial

1. How do you feel about being able to tell the judge what sentence you think your abuser should receive?

2. How do you think you can best figure out what you want to happen to your abuser?

Section 26. Victim Impact Statement

1. How do you feel about the abuse that happened to you? How do you feel about your abuser?
2. What have been the effects of the abuse on your life so far?
3. What do you want your abuser's sentence to be?
4. How will writing (or not writing) a victim impact statement be helpful to you?

Section 27. Sentencing

1. What was the day of the sentencing like for you?
2. How do you think you will feel when you hear the prosecutor say negative things about your abuser and the defense attorney say positive things about your abuser?
3. How do you feel about helping to make sure that your abuser is held responsible for his or her abusive behavior?
4. How do you feel about helping to protect other kids?

Section 28. Toward Recovery

1. How do you feel about forgiving your abuser?
2. What do you want people to know about the experience you have been through? About the abuse? About the trial?
3. What do you want people to know about how these experiences have changed you—for better? for worse?
4. Who are the people you want to thank for helping you through this process? What do you want to say to them?

SUPPORT PEOPLE I CAN DEPEND ON

	Name	Telephone #
Therapist/Counselor	_____	_____
24-Hour Crisis Line	_____	_____
Victim Witness Advocate	_____	_____
Child Interview Specialist	_____	_____
Assistant District Attorney	_____	_____
Police Officer	_____	_____
Doctor	_____	_____
Friend	_____	_____
Friend	_____	_____

HOW IT HAPPENED FOR ME: A DIAGRAM

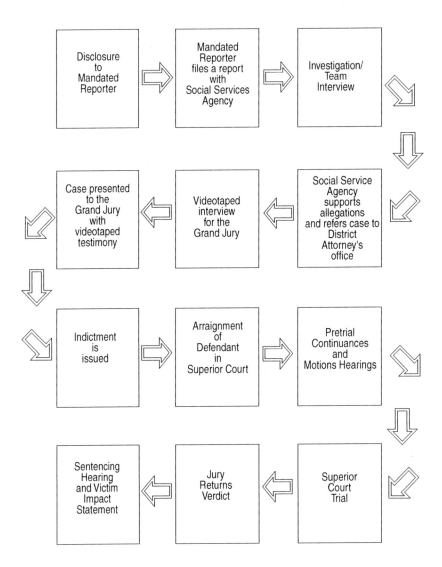

Glossary

acquitted: The charges against the defendant have been dismissed. Most often, if a defendant is acquitted, it is as a result of the jury finding the defendant "not guilty."

ADA: Assistant District Attorney.

allegation: A stated or written accusation by a victim of what happened.

arraignment: The beginning step of the trial proceedings. The defendant comes to court and is formally read the charges.

assistant district attorney (ADA): Lawyer or prosecutor who works for the state (or commonwealth) and represents the state (or commonwealth) on behalf of a crime victim. (*Note:* Check in the following list to see what the prosecuting attorney is called in your state.) *Alabama,* District Attorney; *Alaska,* District Attorney; *Arizona,* County Attorney; *Arkansas,* Prosecuting Attorney; *California,* District Attorney; *Colorado,* District Attorney; *Connecticut,* State's Attorney; *Delaware,* Attorney General; *District of Columbia (Washington, D.C.),* U.S. Attorney; *Florida,* State Attorney; *Georgia,* District Attorney; *Hawaii,* Prosecuting Attorney; *Idaho,* Prosecuting Attorney; *Illinois,* State's Attorney; *Indiana,* Prosecuting Attorney; *Iowa,* County Attorney; *Kansas,* District Attorney or County Attorney; *Kentucky,* Commonwealth's Attorney or County Attorney; *Louisiana,* District Attorney; *Maine,* District Attorney; *Maryland,* State's Attorney; *Massachusetts,* District Attorney; *Michigan,* Prosecuting Attorney; *Minnesota,* County Attorney; *Mississippi,* District Attorney or County Attorney; *Missouri,* Prosecuting Attorney; *Montana,* County Attorney; *Nebraska,* County Attorney; *Nevada,* District Attorney; *New Hampshire,* County Attorney; *New Jersey,* County Prosecutor; *New Mexico,* District Attorney; *New York,* District Attorney; *North Carolina,* District Attorney; *North Dakota,* State's Attorney; *Ohio,* Prosecuting Attorney; *Oklahoma,* District Attorney; *Oregon,*

District Attorney; *Pennsylvania,* District Attorney; *Rhode Island,* Attorney General; *South Carolina,* Circuit Solicitor; *South Dakota,* State's Attorney; *Tennessee,* District Attorney General; *Texas,* Criminal District Attorney or County/District Attorney or District Attorney or County Attorney; *Utah,* County Attorney; *Vermont,* State's Attorney; *Virginia,* Commonwealth's Attorney; *Washington,* County Prosecuting Attorney; *West Virginia,* County Prosecuting Attorney; *Wisconsin,* County District Attorney; *Wyoming,* District Attorney or County Attorney or Prosecuting Attorney. (*National Directory of Prosecuting Attorneys,* 2001. Arlington, VA: National District Attorneys Association, pp. 89-97).

bail: The amount of money posted as a guarantee that the defendant will appear in court on all of the specified court dates.

bail hearing: Hearing in court before a judge to decide whether bail should be posted or whether a defendant can be released on his or her own personal recognizance.

burden of proof: By law, the prosecution is completely responsible for proving a defendant guilty in court "beyond a reasonable doubt." The defendant does not have to prove that he or she is innocent, does not have to testify, and does not even have to have any witnesses testify.

character witness: A person (such as a relative, friend, or employer) who knows the defendant well enough to testify about his or her character; that is about what a good person he or she is and what positive traits he or she has (such as honesty, loyalty, compassion, etc.).

child interview specialist: A person trained to ask children and teenagers questions about what happened in a skillful and sensitive way.

closing arguments: The arguments presented by the prosecutor and the defense attorney at the end of the trial. Each lawyer attempts to convince the jury how to decide based on the evidence presented.

complaining witness: The victim.

continuance: A decision by the court to review the case at a later date.

convicted: The defendant has been found guilty as charged by a jury or a judge.

counselor: A helping professional who listens to you and provides support and information about your feelings.

court officers: Officers of the court who make sure the court operates in an orderly way. Like police officers, the court officers wear uniforms and make sure that all the people in court remain safe.

court reporter: The person who makes a record of everything said in the courtroom. The record can be made by speaking into a machine or by typing into a machine, or both.

credibility: The issue of whether or not an individual's statements are believable.

criminal justice system: A system of government consisting of different types of professionals (judges, district attorneys, police officers, parole and probation officers, victim witness advocates, child interview specialists) which is designed to protect the public, and to work with both victims and perpetrators of crimes.

crisis line: A twenty-four-hour emergency telephone service providing support, counseling and information.

cross-examine: An opportunity for the opposing lawyer to ask a witness questions about evidence which has already been presented to the court.

defendant: The person charged with committing a crime.

defense attorney: A lawyer who represents the defendant.

deliberate: When the jury goes into a private room after a trial is over and discusses all of the evidence from the trial, and decides the verdict. A superior court jury needs to be unanimous in their decision, which means that all twelve jurors must agree on the same verdict.

disclosure: A statement made by a person relating the details of an incident or incidents of abuse.

disposition: The final outcome of a court case. This word often refers to the sentence a defendant receives.

DSS (Department of Social Services): Agency mandated by the Commonwealth of Massachusetts to receive and respond to reports of child abuse and neglect, to provide protection to children, and to provide services to children and their families. (*Note:* Check in the following list to see what the child protective agency is called in your state.) *Alabama,* Office of Protective Services; Adult, Child and Family Services Division; Department of Human Resources; *Alaska,* Division of Family and Youth Services; Department of Health and Social Services; *Arizona,* Administration for Children, Youth and Families; Department of Economic Security; *Arkansas,* Division of Children and Family Services; Department of Human Services; *California,* Department of Social Services; *Colorado,* Department of Human Services; *Connecticut,* Division of Children and Protective Services; Department of Children and Families; *Delaware,* Division of Family Services; Department of Services to Children, Youth, and Their Families; *District of Columbia,* Child and Family Services; Department of Human Services; *Florida,* Department of Children and Family; *Georgia,* Division of Children and Family Services; Department of Human Resources; *Guam,* Child Protective Services, Child Welfare Services; Department of Public Health and Social Services; *Hawaii,* Family and Adult Services; Department of Human Services; *Idaho,* Division of Family and Community Services; Department of Health and Welfare; *Illinois,* Department of Children and Family Services; *Indiana,* Family and Social Services Administration; *Iowa,* Adult, Children and Family Services; Department of Human Services; *Kansas,* Children and Family Services; Department of Social and Rehabilitative Services; *Kentucky,* Department for Protection and Family Support; Cabinet for Families and Children; *Louisiana,* Department of Social Services; *Maine,* Child Protective Services; Department of Human Services; *Maryland,* Child Protective Services; Department of Human Resources; *Massachusetts,* Department of Social Services; *Michigan,* Child Protective Services Division; Department of Social Services; *Minnesota,* Department of Human Services; *Mississippi,* Child Protective Services Unit; Division of Family and Children's Services; Department of Human Services; *Missouri,* Division of Family Services; Department of Social Services; *Montana,* Child and Family Services Division; Department of Public Health and Human Services; *Nebraska,* Department of Health and Human Services; *Nevada,* Division of Child and Family Services; Department of Human Resources; *New Hampshire,* Division for Children, Youth, and Families; Department of Health and Human Services; *New Jersey,* Division of Youth and Family Services; *New*

Mexico, Children, Youth and Families Department; *New York,* Division of Family and Children Services; Department of Social Services; *North Carolina,* Child Protective Services; Division of Social Services; Department of Human Resources; *North Dakota,* Child Protection Services; Department of Human Services; *Ohio,* Office of Child Care and Family Services; Department of Human Services; *Oklahoma,* Division of Children, Youth, and Family; Department of Human Services; *Oregon,* Child Protective Services; State Office for Services to Children and Families; Department of Human Resources; *Pennsylvania,* Office of Children, Youth, and Families; Department of Public Welfare; *Puerto Rico,* Families with Children Program; Department of Social Services; *Rhode Island,* Division of Child Protective Services; Department of Children, Youth, and Families; *South Carolina,* Child Protective Services; Department of Social Services; *South Dakota,* Child Protection Services; Department of Social Services; *Tennessee,* Child Protective Services; Department of Children's Services, Department of Human Services; *Texas,* Department of Protective and Regulatory Services; Department of Human Services; *Utah,* Division of Family Services; Department of Human Services; *Vermont,* Department of Social and Rehabilitative Services; *Virgin Islands,* Division of Children, Youth, and Families; Department of Human Services; *Virginia,* Child Protective Services; Department of Social Services; *Washington,* Child Protective Services; Children's Administration; Department of Social and Health Services; *West Virginia,* Office of Social Services; Department of Health and Human Resources; *Wisconsin,* Child Protective Services; Division of Children and Family Services; Department of Health and Social Services; *Wyoming,* Department of Family Services (U.S. Department of Health and Human Services, 1992; U.S. Department of Health and Human Services, 1998).

empaneling: To select a jury.

Fifth Amendment: The United States Constitution provides rights to people accused of crimes. One of those rights, which is contained in the Fifth Amendment, states that persons accused of crimes do not have to say anything that could be used against them in court.

grand jury: A group of up to twenty-three people who hear evidence and decide whether or not there is reasonable cause to believe a crime happened. Twelve members of the grand jury (a majority) must agree that there is reasonable cause.

guilty: A determination which indicates that the state prosecutor has successfully presented the facts in a way that met the burden of proof beyond a reasonable doubt.

guilty as charged: The decision of the jury that the defendant is guilty of the particular charge specified by the indictment.

indictment: The name used for the formal criminal charge against the defendant.

interview: A meeting with a child interview specialist to talk about what happened.

investigation: The process during which professionals from different disciplines (therapists, child interview specialists, social workers, lawyers, police officers) gather the facts about what happened.

judge: The person who is authorized to hear cases in court and make sure the court is run in an orderly manner.

judge's clerk: The judge's assistant. The clerk sits at a desk in front of the judge and helps the judge run the court by swearing people in as witnesses, keeping track of case documents, and reading verdicts.

jury: A group of up to sixteen people who listen to the facts of the case. Twelve selected jurors will then decide if the defendant is guilty of the charges beyond a reasonable doubt.

mandated reporter: A number of professionals including doctors, therapists, teachers, police officers, foster parents, guidance counselors, or any other person who cares for or works with children in any public or private facility.

mandated reporting law: Requires certain professionals (known as mandated reporters) to file a report when, in his or her professional capacity, he or she has reasonable cause to suspect that a child under the age of eighteen (age varies by state) has been or is being physically or sexually abused or neglected. (*Note:* Investigate the mandated reporting law in your state to see who the mandated reporters are and other points of interest in the law. Every state has a mandated reporting law regarding child abuse.)

motions hearings: *See* PRETRIAL CONFERENCES.

not guilty: A determination which indicates that the state prosecutor has not met the burden of proof beyond a reasonable doubt. This determination does not mean the defendant is innocent.

opening statement: The opportunity for both the prosecutor and the defense attorney to present an outline of what they will accomplish during the trial.

plead: To state on the record whether one is guilty or not guilty of the charges.

presumed innocent: Even after a person has been arrested or charged with a crime, the law says that the accused person must be considered innocent until the prosecution proves him or her guilty.

pretrial conferences: Meetings in court to decide what will happen next on the case. The judge, prosecuting attorney, defendant, and defense attorney take part in the conferences. Victims and witnesses do not have to be present in court. There may be several pretrial conference dates scheduled in court before a trial date is finally scheduled.

pretrial motions: Court appearances by both the prosecuting attorney and the defense attorney before the trial begins in order to discuss the preparation of the case with the judge.

probable cause hearing: In states where the grand jury system is not used, this hearing takes place before a judge for the purpose of determining if the prosecuting attorney has enough evidence of the defendant's guilt to move forward to a jury trial.

probation: A kind of sentence in which the defendant is required to follow rules outlined and monitored by a probation officer. For example: having to go to counseling, meeting with a probation officer regularly, staying away from children. Sometimes a defendant is given probation instead of a prison sentence and sometimes probation is given in addition to a prison sentence. If a defendant does not follow the rules of probation, a judge can then order the defendant to go to jail.

prosecution: A process by which the state (commonwealth) brings criminal charges against someone, and then brings a case to trial.

reasonable doubt: Any doubt that a reasonable, responsible person would have a hard time dismissing.

recess: A break in the trial proceedings.

restraining order: An order issued by a judge specifying that one individual be prevented from abusing another individual, and be kept away from and/or removed from the premises of the person who applied for the restraining order.

sequestered: To be separated, so as not to be influenced by the testimony of one another. A jury can also be sequestered so as not to be influenced by the media.

social worker: A professional trained to provide a range of services to families including support and counseling.

statutes: Laws that are created by the state or federal government.

subpoena: A court order sent to a witness, requiring the witness to be present in court. A subpoena can be sent by mail or delivered by hand by a constable, sheriff, or agent of the court.

summons: A written notification issued by the court that orders the defendant to appear in court on a certain day to be arraigned. A summons can be sent by mail or delivered by hand.

superior court: The level of the court system that handles more serious crimes known as felonies. (*Note:* Some child abuse cases are tried in the district court system. This could be because the crime is considered a misdemeanor [which is a less serious crime—like indecent exposure] instead of a felony. District court procedures will differ from those in superior court. If your case is going through the district court system, be sure to ask your victim witness advocate to explain the different procedures.)

supports the allegations: To support an allegation of abuse means that the state social service agency has reasonable cause to believe that an incident of abuse or neglect of a child or teenager did occur.

suspended sentence: A prison sentence that a defendant is not required to serve right away. Instead the defendant is placed on probation with certain rules that must be followed. Usually these rules include sex-offender treatment and no contact with the victim. If the defendant does not follow the rules of probation, he or she could be made to serve the suspended sentence in prison.

team interview: A team of professionals consisting of a social worker, assistant district attorney, victim witness advocate, child interview specialist, police officer, and a therapist who come together to cooperatively conduct an investigation, including observing an interview and discussing what should happen next in the case.

testify: To answer questions in court under the oath to tell the truth.

testimony: A statement made by a witness under oath in response to questions asked by a lawyer.

therapist: A person trained to assist others in dealing with problems or concerns.

verdict: The decision of the jury. In a superior court criminal trial the decision must be unanimous.

victim: The person who is wronged by the crime.

victim impact statement: At the time of sentencing victims and their families can make a written or a verbal statement to the judge about how they feel about what happened, what the effects of the crime are, and what they think the sentence should be. In deciding what sentence a defendant will receive, the judge considers what the prosecuting attorney, the defense attorney, and the victims recommend.

victim witness advocate: A support person who guides victims and witnesses through the court system.

witness: A person who testifies (tells), under oath, what he or she saw or heard happen.

witness stand: The place in court where the witness sits or stands to testify. At this place, usually next to the judge, the witness will be sworn in and will answer questions.

THE HAWORTH MALTREATMENT AND TRAUMA PRESS®
Robert A. Geffner, PhD
Senior Editor

THE INSIDERS: A MAN'S RECOVERY FROM TRAUMATIC CHILDHOOD ABUSE by Robert Blackburn Knight. (2002). "An important book. . . . Fills a gap in the literature about healing from childhood sexual abuse by allowing us to hear, in undiluted terms, about one man's history and journey of recovery." *Amy Pine, MA, LMFT, psychotherapist and co-founder, Survivors Healing Center, Santa Cruz, California*

WE ARE NOT ALONE: A GUIDEBOOK FOR HELPING PROFESSIONALS AND PARENTS SUPPORTING ADOLESCENT VICTIMS OF SEXUAL ABUSE by Jade Christine Angelica. (2002). "Encourages victims and their families to participate in the system in an effort to heal from their victimization, seek justice, and hold offenders accountable for their crimes. An exceedingly vital training tool." *Janet Fine, MS, Director, Victim Witness Assistance Program and Children's Advocacy Center, Suffolk County District Attorney's Office, Boston*

WE ARE NOT ALONE: A TEENAGE GIRL'S PERSONAL ACCOUNT OF INCEST FROM DISCLOSURE THROUGH PROSECUTION AND TREATMENT by Jade Christine Angelica. (2002). "A valuable resource for teens who have been sexually abused and their parents. With compassion and eloquent prose, Angelica walks people through the criminal justice system—from disclosure to final outcome." *Kathleen Kendall-Tackett, PhD, Research Associate, Family Research Laboratory, University of New Hampshire, Durham*

WE ARE NOT ALONE: A TEENAGE BOY'S PERSONAL ACCOUNT OF CHILD SEXUAL ABUSE FROM DISCLOSURE THROUGH PROSECUTION AND TREATMENT by Jade Christine Angelica. (2002). "Inspires us to work harder to meet kids' needs, answer their questions, calm their fears, and protect them from their abusers and the system, which is often not designed to respond to them in a language they understand." *Kevin L. Ryle, JD, Assistant District Attorney, Middlesex, Massachusetts*

GROWING FREE: A MANUAL FOR SURVIVORS OF DOMESTIC VIOLENCE by Wendy Susan Deaton and Michael Hertica. (2001). "This is a necessary book for anyone who is scared and starting to think about what it would take to 'grow free.' . . . Very helpful for friends and relatives of a person in a domestic violence situation. I recommend it highly." *Colleen Friend, LCSW, Field Work Consultant, UCLA Department of Social Welfare, School of Public Policy & Social Research*

A THERAPIST'S GUIDE TO **GROWING FREE: A MANUAL FOR SURVIVOR'S OF DOMESTIC VIOLENCE** by Wendy Susan Deaton and Michael Hertica. (2001). "An excellent synopsis of the theories and research behind the manual." *Beatrice Crofts Yorker, RN, JD, Professor of Nursing, Georgia State University, Decatur*

PATTERNS OF CHILD ABUSE: HOW DYSFUNCTIONAL TRANSACTIONS ARE REPLICATED IN INDIVIDUALS, FAMILIES, AND THE CHILD WELFARE SYSTEM by Michael Karson. (2001). "No one interested in what may well be the major public health epidemic of our time in terms of its long-term consequences for our society can afford to pass up the opportunity to read this enlightening work." *Howard Wolowitz, PhD, Professor Emeritus, Psychology Department, University of Michigan, Ann Arbor*

IDENTIFYING CHILD MOLESTERS: PREVENTING CHILD SEXUAL ABUSE BY RECOGNIZING THE PATTERNS OF THE OFFENDERS by Carla van Dam. (2000). "The definitive work on the subject. . . . Provides parents and others with the tools to recognize when and how to intervene." *Roger W. Wolfe, MA, Co-Director, N. W. Treatment Associates, Seattle, Washington*

POLITICAL VIOLENCE AND THE PALESTINIAN FAMILY: IMPLICATIONS FOR MENTAL HEALTH AND WELL-BEING by Vivian Khamis. (2000). "A valuable book . . . a pioneering work that fills a glaring gap in the study of Palestinian society." *Elia Zureik, Professor of Sociology, Queens University, Kingston, Ontario, Canada*

STOPPING THE VIOLENCE: A GROUP MODEL TO CHANGE MEN'S ABUSIVE ATTITUDES AND BEHAVIORS by David J. Decker. (1999). "A concise and thorough manual to assist clinicians in learning the causes and dynamics of domestic violence." *Joanne Kittel, MSW, LICSW, Yachats, Oregon*

STOPPING THE VIOLENCE: A GROUP MODEL TO CHANGE MEN'S ABUSIVE ATTITUDES AND BEHAVIORS, THE CLIENT WORKBOOK by David J. Decker. (1999).

BREAKING THE SILENCE: GROUP THERAPY FOR CHILDHOOD SEXUAL ABUSE, A PRACTITIONER'S MANUAL by Judith A. Margolin. (1999). "This book is an extremely valuable and well-written resource for all therapists working with adult survivors of child sexual abuse." *Esther Deblinger, PhD, Associate Professor of Clinical Psychiatry, University of Medicine and Dentistry of New Jersey School of Osteopathic Medicine*

"I NEVER TOLD ANYONE THIS BEFORE": MANAGING THE INITIAL DISCLOSURE OF SEXUAL ABUSE RE-COLLECTIONS by Janice A. Gasker. (1999). "Discusses the elements needed to create a safe, therapeutic environment and offers the practitioner a number of useful strategies for responding appropriately to client disclosure." *Roberta G. Sands, PhD, Associate Professor, University of Pennsylvania School of Social Work*

FROM SURVIVING TO THRIVING: A THERAPIST'S GUIDE TO STAGE II RECOVERY FOR SURVIVORS OF CHILDHOOD ABUSE by Mary Bratton. (1999). "A must read for all, including survivors. Bratton takes a lifelong debilitating disorder and unravels its intricacies in concise, succinct, and understandable language." *Phillip A. Whitner, PhD, Sr. Staff Counselor, University Counseling Center, The University of Toledo, Ohio*

SIBLING ABUSE TRAUMA: ASSESSMENT AND INTERVENTION STRATEGIES FOR CHILDREN, FAMILIES, AND ADULTS by John V. Caffaro and Allison Conn-Caffaro. (1998). "One area that has almost consistently been ignored in the research and writing on child maltreatment is the area of sibling abuse. This book is a welcome and required addition to the developing literature on abuse." *Judith L. Alpert, PhD, Professor of Applied Psychology, New York University*

BEARING WITNESS: VIOLENCE AND COLLECTIVE RESPONSIBILITY by Sandra L. Bloom and Michael Reichert. (1998). "A totally convincing argument. . . . Demands careful study by all elected representatives, the clergy, the mental health and medical professions, representatives of the media, and all those unwittingly involved in this repressive perpetuation and catastrophic global problem." *Harold I. Eist, MD, Past President, American Psychiatric Association*

TREATING CHILDREN WITH SEXUALLY ABUSIVE BEHAVIOR PROBLEMS: GUIDELINES FOR CHILD AND PARENT INTERVENTION by Jan Ellen Burton, Lucinda A. Rasmussen, Julie Bradshaw, Barbara J. Christopherson, and Steven C. Huke. (1998). "An extremely readable book that is well-documented and a mine of valuable 'hands on' information. . . . This is a book that all those who work with sexually abusive children or want to work with them must read." *Sharon K. Araji, PhD, Professor of Sociology, University of Alaska, Anchorage*

THE LEARNING ABOUT MYSELF (LAMS) PROGRAM FOR AT-RISK PARENTS: LEARNING FROM THE PAST—CHANGING THE FUTURE by Verna Rickard. (1998). "This program should be a part of the resource materials of every mental health professional trusted with the responsibility of working with 'at-risk' parents." *Terry King, PhD, Clinical Psychologist, Federal Bureau of Prisons, Catlettsburg, Kentucky*

THE LEARNING ABOUT MYSELF (LAMS) PROGRAM FOR AT-RISK PARENTS: HANDBOOK FOR GROUP PARTICIPANTS by Verna Rickard. (1998). "Not only is the LAMS program designed to be educational and build skills for future use, it is also fun!" *Martha Morrison Dore, PhD, Associate Professor of Social Work, Columbia University, New York, New York*

BRIDGING WORLDS: UNDERSTANDING AND FACILITATING ADOLESCENT RECOVERY FROM THE TRAUMA OF ABUSE by Joycee Kennedy and Carol McCarthy. (1998). "An extraordinary survey of the history of child neglect and abuse in America. . . . A wonderful teaching tool at the university level, but should be required reading in high schools as well." *Florabel Kinsler, PhD, BCD, LCSW, Licensed Clinical Social Worker, Los Angeles, California*

CEDAR HOUSE: A MODEL CHILD ABUSE TREATMENT PROGRAM by Bobbi Kendig with Clara Lowry. (1998). "Kendig and Lowry truly . . . realize the saying that we are our brothers' keepers. Their spirit permeates this volume, and that spirit of caring is what always makes the difference for people in painful situations." *Hershel K. Swinger, PhD, Clinical Director, Children's Institute International, Los Angeles, California*

SEXUAL, PHYSICAL, AND EMOTIONAL ABUSE IN OUT-OF-HOME CARE: PREVENTION SKILLS FOR AT-RISK CHILDREN by Toni Cavanagh Johnson and Associates. (1997). "Professionals who make dispositional decisions or who are related to out-of-home care for children could benefit from reading and following the curriculum of this book with children in placements." *Issues in Child Abuse Accusations*

Order Your Own Copy of
This Important Book for Your Personal Library!

WE ARE NOT ALONE
A Teenage Girl's Personal Account of Incest
from Disclosure Through Prosecution and Treatment

_____in softbound at $14.95 (ISBN: 0-7890-0926-9)

COST OF BOOKS_____

OUTSIDE USA/CANADA/
MEXICO: ADD 20%____

POSTAGE & HANDLING_____
*(US: $4.00 for first book & $1.50
for each additional book)*
*Outside US: $5.00 for first book
& $2.00 for each additional book)*

SUBTOTAL_____

in Canada: add 7% GST____

STATE TAX____
*(NY, OH & MIN residents, please
add appropriate local sales tax)*

FINAL TOTAL____
*(If paying in Canadian funds,
convert using the current
exchange rate, UNESCO
coupons welcome.)*

❏ **BILL ME LATER:** ($5 service charge will be added)
(Bill-me option is good on US/Canada/Mexico orders only;
not good to jobbers, wholesalers, or subscription agencies.)

❏ Check here if billing address is different from
shipping address and attach purchase order and
billing address information.

Signature_____

❏ **PAYMENT ENCLOSED: $_____**

❏ **PLEASE CHARGE TO MY CREDIT CARD.**

❏ Visa ❏ MasterCard ❏ AmEx ❏ Discover
❏ Diner's Club ❏ Eurocard ❏ JCB

Account # _____

Exp. Date_____

Signature_____

Prices in US dollars and subject to change without notice.

NAME_____

INSTITUTION_____

ADDRESS_____

CITY_____

STATE/ZIP_____

COUNTRY_____ COUNTY (NY residents only)_____

TEL_____ FAX_____

E-MAIL_____

May we use your e-mail address for confirmations and other types of information? ❏ Yes ❏ No
We appreciate receiving your e-mail address and fax number. Haworth would like to e-mail or fax special
discount offers to you, as a preferred customer. **We will never share, rent, or exchange your e-mail address
or fax number.** We regard such actions as an invasion of your privacy.

Order From Your Local Bookstore or Directly From
The Haworth Press, Inc.
10 Alice Street, Binghamton, New York 13904-1580 • USA
TELEPHONE: 1-800-HAWORTH (1-800-429-6784) / Outside US/Canada: (607) 722-5857
FAX: 1-800-895-0582 / Outside US/Canada: (607) 722-6362
E-mail: getinfo@haworthpressinc.com
PLEASE PHOTOCOPY THIS FORM FOR YOUR PERSONAL USE.
www.HaworthPress.com

BOF00